HOMO MYSTICUS

Three Lectures

Wolfgang Struve

Translated by George Wald

University Press of America,® Inc.
Lanham · Boulder · New York · Toronto · Plymouth, UK

These lectures were originally published in German as
Homo Mysticus: Zwei Vorträge by Anders Leben Verlag © 1983
and as *Über die Nichtkonformität des Wirklichen* by
Anders Leben Verlag © 1986.

English translation © 2015 by George Wald

University Press of America,® Inc.
4501 Forbes Boulevard
Suite 200
Lanham, Maryland 20706
UPA Acquisitions Department (301) 459-3366

Unit A, Whitacre Mews, 26-34 Stannary Street,
London SE11 4AB, United Kingdom

All rights reserved

British Library Cataloging in Publication Information Available

Library of Congress Control Number: 2013957265
ISBN: 978-0-7618-6322-9 (paperback : alk. paper)
eISBN: 978-0-7618-6323-6

Cover artwork depicts the area around Le Catogne mountain in
Champex, Valais, Switzerland.

Author and translator photograph by Ursula Schneider.

U. S.

Diu meiste sache ist, daz der mensche muoz durchgân und übergân alliu dinc und aller dinge ursache, und dis beginnet den menschen verdriezen. Dâ von blîbet der mensche in sîner kleinheit.

Meister Eckhart

["The main thing is that man must pass through and pass beyond everything and the cause of everything, and this begins man's vexation. This is why man lags behind in his feebleness."]

Contents

Translator's Introduction   vii

World and Reality
Reflections on an Elementary Distinction in Philosophy   1

Mysticism East and West and the Problem of Absolute
Transcendence   21

On the Nonconformity of the Real   43

Select Bibliography of Publications by Wolfgang Struve   65

References   69

Translator's Introduction

The thoughts in the following three lectures have become exceedingly rare. Yet it is thoughts like these that our technological and informational age is desperately in need of. Wolfgang Struve, who delivered these lectures over a period of ten years, spent a lifetime meditating on these thoughts, and these are the fruit of that meditation, the distillation of his life's preoccupation.

Struve is for the most part unknown in the English-speaking world, though he did once speak at Vassar College in Poughkeepsie, New York, and a few of his students are in America.[1] This translation is intended to begin to make Struve known to English speakers. Born in Hamburg in 1917, he came to Freiburg in the south of Germany, and also to Zürich, Switzerland, to study philosophy, physics and mathematics. In Freiburg he met Martin Heidegger, who, after having heard Struve's first paper, took him on as a doctoral candidate. This relationship, as Struve reports in the second of these lectures, continued until Heidegger's death. That Heidegger took him on as a doctoral candidate indicates the high esteem he held Struve in, for though many were regular students in Heidegger's lecture courses and seminars, very few actually wrote dissertations under him.[2] Struve produced a dissertation on Aristotle's *Physics* in 1943, earn-

---

[1] There are the late Joan Stambaugh, his first doctoral candidate, who wrote *Untersuchungen zum Problem der Zeit bei Nietzsche*, which was reviewed by Karl Löwith, the late William S. Wurzer, who wrote *Nietzsche und Spinoza*, and I, who wrote a master's thesis on Schelling's *Ages of the World* and a doctoral dissertation on the transformation of the Platonic ideas and identity in the light of the ascent in Plotinus. Other students include: Abdel-Ghaffar Mikkawy, *Philosophische Untersuchung zum Begriff des Absurden und der Revolte bei Albert Camus*, Hermann Josef Schmidt, *Nietzsche und Sokrates*, Till Beckmann, *Studien zur Bestimmung des Lebens in Meister Eckharts deutschen Predigten*, Ursula Schneider, *Grundzüge einer Philosophie des Glücks bei Nietzsche*, Anselm Model, *Metaphysik und reflektierende Urteilskraft bei Kant*, and Sung-Jin Kim, *Der Widerspruch und das Urteil in Platons "Parmenides."* The diversity of topics covered here indicates the wide range of philosophers whom Struve felt at home with.

[2] Decades later, Heidegger wrote Struve that already then he had placed a "circled one" next to his name. This was reported by Rudolf Brandner, who had it from conversation with Struve, in "Die Rehabilitation philosophischer Mystik: Zum Gedankenwerk des Philosophen und Mystikers Wolfgang Struve," *Mesotes*, 3, no. 2 (1993), p. 250.

ing his doctorate *summa cum laude* during a four-month leave from the War, into which he had been drafted. After the war was over, he made a narrow escape from the Soviet prisoner of war camp by a daring swim across the Elba to the American side. Soon afterwards he was able to return to the university and to begin work on his *Habilitationsschrift*[3] on Kierkegaard and Nietzsche. The influence that Kierkegaard exercised in Germany in the early part of the 20th century—notably on Karl Jaspers and Martin Heidegger—had been through translations which were somewhat loose and in places watered down. Struve learned Danish in a very short time and made a thorough study not only of the famous works, but of the journals and papers, which were mostly untranslated at that time. He made the first translation into German of *Johannes Climacus eller de omnibus dubitandum est.*[4] Struve taught at the University of Freiburg starting in 1948 and received a professorship in 1955 after submitting a still unpublished book on Plotinus. He retired in 1981. In the realm of textual interpretation, I think Heidegger's care and extreme attentiveness in approaching the history of philosophy are evident in all Struve's studies of the great philosophers in lecture courses and publications as well as in the reflections on them in his own thought. Indeed, Struve said on a number of occasions in lecture courses that Heidegger's greatness lay in his having so clearly shown the difference between ancient and modern ways of thinking. But even here, where Struve, especially in his first book, *Die neuzeitliche Philosophie als Metaphysik der Subjektivität: Interpretationen zu Kierkegaard und Nietzsche,* might be seen to be carrying on Heidegger's "destruction" of the history of philosophy, he differs from his famous doctoral advisor in what things he is looking for in the great texts of the history of philosophy, not to mention that Struve sees no grandiose *Seinsgeschichte,* or "history of being," in these texts. And the difference from his advisor becomes totally apparent in his own thought, which seems to belong to an entirely different world. For Heidegger calls the "whither" of transcendence *world* and says he will "now define transcendence as *being-in-the-world,*"[5] which in the end is a denial or at any rate severe limitation of transcendence. Struve is interested in leaving the world; world is just what is to be transcended, but ultimately simply left, as said. Indeed, as we shall see, he calls the real the "not of the world." This alone makes what Struve has to say difficult to understand because it goes against the current of the time. Heidegger, to his credit and in distinction from many German professors of philosophy, tolerated philosophical difference from himself and continued to support Struve even after this difference became apparent. Years later, when Struve sent Heidegger his aphorisms

---

[3] A sort of second doctorate—a number of countries, such as France and Denmark, have a similar system—granting *venia legendi,* or the right to hold lectures.
[4] *Johannes Climacus oder de omnibus dubitandum est* (Darmstadt: Claasen & Würth, 1948). Similarly, Ludwig Wittgenstein, whose *Tractatus Logico-Philosophicus* Struve held a seminar on in the winter semester of 1958/59, also read Kierkegaard in Danish.
[5] "Vom Wesen des Grundes" in *Wegmarken* (Frankfurt: Klostermann, 1967), p. 35.

on Egypt,[6] Heidegger was extremely fascinated. Among these texts was the following:

> The *Logos*—"the huge advance of the Greeks over the Egyptians": no one would want to dispute that; the question is only where to and away from what this advancement was.[7]

Though the *logos* is the mode of thought we have in the West, Struve's ultimate concern is not the *logos*. Nonetheless, Struve is eminently logical in his thought; as he says, logic brought to its height is dialectics, and he proves himself to be a consummate dialectician in these lectures. Though he does say in one of the lectures that mysticism is irrational in tendency, we must not take "irrational" in the sense of a revolt against reason which would therefore remain ultimately rational by its being tied to the rational by its very denial of the rational—here he means that mysticism is non-rational. Simply, it does not take reason as the highest value. For it is Struve's view that in order for what defies thought to become manifest, thought must itself become totally clear and free itself from all the illusions we create for ourselves. A thinking that doesn't lose sight of anything essential proves itself to be very rigorous; such a thinking is also necessarily very intense. He has many times alluded to the opening of the chapter "The Absolute Paradox" in Kierkegaard's *Philosophical Tidbits*: "But the highest pitch of every passion is always to will its own downfall; and so it is also the supreme passion of the understanding to seek a collision, though this collision must in one way or another prove its undoing. This, then, is the supreme paradox of all thought, to want to discover something that thought itself cannot think."[8] Seeking such a "collision"[9] might be said to be a *Leitmotif* in Struve's thinking. We find this passion in every word of these lectures, and the

---

[6] First published in the journal *Antaios*, 1964, subsequently in Struve's book *Der andere Zug* (Salzburg-München: Stifterbibliothek, 1967/69) under the title "Groszheit," pp. 257-274. Struve writes most of his philosophy in the form of aphorisms—or what he more recently preferred calling "short texts" or simply "notes"—in journals from which he has from time to time made a selection and published as a book.

[7] *Der andere Zug*, p. 259.

[8] *Philosophical Fragments*, translated by David Swenson, revised by Howard V. Hong (Princeton: Princeton University Press, 1936/1962), p. 46, blending it with Howard V. Hong and Edna H. Hong's more literal translation (Princeton: Princeton University Press, 1985), p. 37 (*S.V.* 204). Other possible English translations of the Danish word *smuler* are: *"scraps," "morsels," "crumbs."* Walter Lowrie used the Reverend William M. Weber's "tidbits" as soon as he heard it, previously having used "scraps," which also allowed him to reproduce the word play on *Smuler* and *Smule: Philosophical Tidbits and a Bit of Philosophy Too* (see *The Concept of Dread*, translated by Lowrie, Princeton: Princeton University Press, 1944, p. v.). That my cousin's Swedish wife, who is not versed in philosophy, offered "tidbits" as the first thing that came to mind for *smuler* would seem to confirm Weber and Lowrie. Struve once proposed as a translation of the title: *Philosophische Stücke oder ein Stück Philosophie*.

[9] *Anstød* in Kierkegaard, *Stoß* in Struve, which I have generally translated "running up against."

thought developed here with such great incisiveness and eloquence carries the reader on and takes him up in a strong current which is at once fascinating and intoxicating. Yet it lets us see clearly what is contained in the concepts we use. If the reader is attentive, he may be brought to the verge of a "collision," such as we just spoke of. And this is something that no literature I know of today does. We are used to participating in a stream of collective consciousness and of acting and reacting within this stream: so very few writers or artists point us away from this collective consciousness. Indeed, most authors revel in participating in this collective consciousness, in the ongoing public discussion that the world carries on with itself. Another stream, perhaps coming from the place that the *logos* moves us away from, makes itself felt here. Because Struve has found a level where division into the categories of the religious and the philosophical doesn't apply, he "has remained a stranger" and an outsider to contemporary philosophy.[10]

At the same time, these lectures give us the terrain of Struve's thought. Each lecture has a different emphasis and approaches its subject matter from a different angle. The series of lectures also represents perhaps not so much a development of his thought—in a sense his basic insight has been there from the beginning—but further deepenings of his thought along with changing vocabulary. The main theme of these lectures is what he calls in the second lecture "absolute transcendence," and each lecture takes up this theme anew with a different starting point.

His point of departure in these lectures is the conventional—indeed, basic words in these lectures are a concession to convention, for example, "mysticism," "absolute transcendence"—in this way he can connect to our everyday thinking and thus make it possible for us to follow him into what is totally unconventional in thought. And so each of the lectures begins with a discussion of terms. But from here he leads us into dialectical trains of thought that can be difficult to follow if one is unused to them. He states in the third lecture that reflection excludes the absolute, and thus so does most contemporary thought. The absolute, he says, can only be spoken of naïvely or dialectically. These lectures, in moving between these modes of thought, are unique in current philosophical thought.

His topic, he says, requires "an ongoing reflection on its method of treatment, and its justification." This means also reflection on the form of philosophy. He has said that Kierkegaard and Nietzsche have brought a new honesty into philosophy that renders dishonest any attempts subsequent to them to construct a system in the manner of the great German idealists or to present philosophy in the form of learned treatises in the manner of what Karl Jaspers called the *Professorenphilosophie* of the second half of the nineteenth century and beyond. Philosophy can no longer be done in that form.—

Furthermore, as in all true philosophical thought, there is an "existential" demand that we enter into the thought with all our being, that we must also

---

[10] See the second lecture below, "Mysticism East and West," p. 24.

sharpen our senses for everything going on around us and within ourselves even before attending to certain elemental distinctions made in thought:

> Most of the time we are only occupied intellectually, not actually active inwardly.—Actual inward activity: the directing of the *entire* man towards the real. *This* directing occurs without conceptual thought, precedes all our conceptuality.[11]

It is essential that we be aware of what is going on inwardly in order to be able to make sense out of and lend reality to our conceptions—intellectual thought must put down roots in a soil in order for it to mean anything. We must "understand the abstract concretely." True philosophical thought must indeed be rigorously intellectual, but it also demands a total engagement.

Struve regards "World and Reality: Reflections on an Elementary Distinction in Philosophy," as a kind of basic statement of his thought, and indeed it has sparked some interest, the text having appeared on the Internet. He says that "what characterizes the thought about to be communicated here is the way in which the concept of transcendence will emerge and be intensified to the utmost." He begins with a discussion of the concepts of "world" and reality. He makes it clear that he "does not, however, purport to set up or develop a theory—be it a new one or an old one—of world and reality." These concepts are identical for most of us, but we come to see them through a series of dialectical trains of thought as fundamentally distinct. In characterizing the distinction and the relation between world and reality, he delineates two "figures of thought." The first figure distinguishes origin and what arises from this origin. We know this in many variations throughout our history. There is some ultimate *ground,* whether God, the First Principle, or whatever, and there is what derives from this. Struve describes a dialectic of origin and what arises from it: origin and what arises from it must be both distinct from each other and also the same; they must be mutually dependent on each other; and the origin must have primacy over what arises from it. This dialectic is not a construction of Struve's; rather, this dialectic is what Struve sees as logically contained in the concept of origin. The origin, here conceived as "what is other than world," remains in a relation to world and is therefore something "relatively transcendent." This concept is basically philosophical. It can also be found in Eastern thought, in, for instance, the concept of Brahma. It is the Primordial One of Neoplatonism. It is the God who creates the universe. The various moments of this dialectic become radicalized in philosophies oriented towards mysticism, so that, for instance, our sameness with or difference from the origin are thought through in a consequent manner and we are one with the origin, or the origin is infinitely different. Over against this Struve delineates a second figure of thought which describes another kind of transcendence, one in which the relation of world to what is other than world is conceived as that of illusion to reality. In this figure of thought world is seen to

---

[11] Wolfgang Struve, *Übergehn zur Wirklichkeit: Philosophische und andere Reisenotizen* (Salzburg: Stifterbibliothek, 1970), p. 61.

be not real in the face of what is other than world. Here world and reality have nothing to do with one another. Here what is other than world is something "absolutely transcendent." This concept is difficult to think and is not as obvious as it may seem after we have heard it and perhaps believe that we have always known it.

Struve develops the idea of "something absolutely transcendent" dialectically by conceiving what is other than the world as the "not of the world." We resist this somewhat, because the current philosophical climate prefers oneness and eschews any sort of dualism. The not of the world negates not only everything finite, but it also negates the null. And so we come to see the not of the world as something "infinitely higher than . . . the world."

In conversation in a small group in a restaurant after its delivery in Freiburg, Struve said that what is "new" in this lecture is that the real as the not of the world is experienced in nature. Indeed, in an earlier book, he had said,

> "Not of the world" and similar speculative-dialectical concepts at first seem to be mere operations in thought. And they would be that if nature weren't in certain places, namely, where it is not cultivatable, as it were penetrated by an other.
>
> And I do not come upon this through logical operations, rather, that magic in nature compels me to these thoughts, carries and nourishes them and makes them real.[12]

The words "magic" and "magical" come up a lot in his writings at this time when he talks about nature. He uses them to point to a quality that makes nature point beyond itself, to the real, to something transcendent. He suggests its meaning in one place:

> What I call the "magical" does not in any way coincide with the beautiful, let alone with the spectacular. One of its main characteristics is that it impresses itself upon me more than anything else.—[13]

Struve feels that as finite beings we cannot simply encounter the real without something concretely there; we cannot simply "conjure up" the real:

> And this too is clear: all mysticism takes its point of departure from the senses, not from the intellect.[14]

Maybe at some time in the past, when we lived more closely with nature, it would not have to have been emphasized so much that the real is encountered in nature or, more precisely, "directly with respect to" nature *("unmittelbar an der*

---

[12] *Unglaubliche Wirklichkeit: Philosophische und andere Reisenotizen.* (Salzburg: Stifterbibliothek, 1972), p. 53.
[13] *Unglaubliche Wirklichkeit*, p. 102f.
[14] *Der andere Zug*, p. 52. See also *Unglaubliche Wirklichkeit*, pp. 115: "For reality is *not* all that which you are and which the world is. This not is embodied only in nature devoid of all human beings."

Natur"[15]*)*. Nature "is not reality, but nature is its 'neighbor.'"[16] But in today's world, where, in the West at least, almost every remote corner has been covered with and penetrated by a net of technological devices and systems, getting access to nature takes on a paramount importance.

In earlier writings he tended to talk about the "turn inward" in the Plotinian sense, or in terms of the "inwardness" of Kierkegaard. Now, coincident with his thought of "absolute transcendence," Struve says, "But the real is only outdoors.—"[17] He does not really change his mind about this; rather, it is a change of emphasis. There is a type of introspection which is really more of a getting caught up with oneself than true inward seeing:

> "I am my life." The real can therefore only be found outside me in momentary touch. Withdrawal into oneself is the root of all perversion.[18]

The other is also what is "primally one's own" by a dialectic of sorts:

> *I* am not real; but: I grasp reality only in me, and that means at the same time— because of the "*coincidentia oppositorum*"—only outside myself.[19]

We must indeed be looking within and seeing what is happening there, seeing everything that is going on, but this inward looking must not become something obsessive or be sidetracked by being carried away by some thought which proves itself to be illusion. It is just as important to see everything that is going on outside oneself, to be aware of everything.

Struve is not advocating some sort of nature romanticism such as began with some nineteenth century writers in both Germany and America. It is not simply the physical exhilaration we experience while being outdoors in beautiful mountains surrounded by forests and rivers.[20] It is not simply getting close to

---

[15] See *Übergehn zur Wirklichkeit*, p. 75.
[16] *Unglaubliche Wirklichkeit*, p. 117
[17] *Übergehn zur Wirklichkeit*, p. 34.
[18] *Spuren und Stürze: Aufzeichnungen aus Skizzenbüchern 1984-1987*. With 4 watercolor paintings by the author and an afterword by Ursula Schneider. (Vienna: Passagen, 1999) #48. (I would like to call this book *Tracks and Tumbles* in English.) See also #12: "The point of reality lies outside you. If you place it inside yourself, you are living in illusion."
[19] *Übergehn zur Wirklichkeit: Philosophische und andere Reisenotizen* (Salzburg: Stifterbibliothek/Bad Goisern: Neugebauer Press, 1970), p. 41.
[20] I think Struve might have found D. H. Lawrence's attitude as expressed in *The Captain's Doll* (1923) congenial:

"'Bergheil!' cried a youth with bare arms and bare chest, bare head, terrific fanged boots, a knapsack and an alpenstock, and all the bronzed wind and sun of the mountain snow in his skin and his faintly bleached hair. With his great heavy knapsack, his rumpled thick stockings, his ghastly fanged boots, Hepburn found him repulsive.

"'Guten Tag,' he answered coldly.

"'Grüss Gott,' said Hannele.

"And the young Tannhäuser, the young Siegfried, this young Balder beautiful, strode climbing down the rocks, marching and swinging with his alpenstock."

what is natural while we escape all the devices of our technological civilization. Nature is "worldless"[21] and thus becomes the "sensuous representative" of the real, that is, it "presents it for the senses."[22] And so an absorption in nature, a sort of meditation in nature, becomes essential if we are to be "transported"[23] to the real.

Since very early on Struve had a deep connection to nature. At twenty he traveled to Upper Engadine, Switzerland, and walked into the valley. Before him Nietzsche had wandered off from Sankt Moritz and discovered Sils Maria, at that time unknown to tourists. Nietzsche spent his last several summers there. That both Nietzsche and Struve were so strongly attracted to this region perhaps testifies to the fact that Struve could draw on Nietzsche in new ways because they had in common a fascination for the same types of nature and what could be encountered there. Struve returned over and over again to this region. In the years I first knew him he was renting part of a farmhouse in Fex Valley, which lies above the main valley, and spent a part of each year there. In later years he stayed in Maloja, which is the last village in the main valley before there is a deep drop to the Bregaglia Valley. He wrote many of his aphorisms in this region and also in the Valais area of Switzerland (the area where the Matterhorn is). He leaves us a record of how thought grows out of an experience of nature in two books of aphorisms, *Übergehn zur Wirklichkeit (Passage to Reality)* and *Unglaubliche Wirklichkeit (Incredible Reality)*, both with the same subtitle: *Philosophical and Other Travel Notes*. Aphorisms of a philosophical nature are interspersed between descriptions of the nature he encounters. These are not simply descriptions of landscape as in a travelogue, but "the author cannot speak of a landscape in any other way than so far as it has become an element of thought for him."[24] It is also in these two books that he introduces what in the second of these lectures is called "absolute transcendence." In his last decades he completed one watercolor painting a day, sometimes more, rain or shine, and many of his watercolors are of these two regions of Switzerland. These watercolors more and more replaced his earlier verbal descriptions.[25] In fact, "both, doing watercolors outdoors and meditative thinking, have become for their author in the course of time an inseparable unity."[26]

But Struve did not confine his experience of nature to Switzerland and the Black Forest (on the edge of which he had his apartment in Freiburg). Like

---

See *Unglaubliche Wirklichkeit*, p. 110: "Disturbed somewhat by a troop of young people who came stumbling along the path in the midday heat with ridiculously large packs and with bells on their rucksacks."
[21] See, for instance, *Der andere Zug*, p. 250, and *Unglaubliche Wirklichkeit*, p. 111.
[22] *Unglaubliche Wirklichkeit*, p. 107.
[23] "*Übersetzt*": see p. 14 below.
[24] *Übergehn zur Wirklichkeit*, p. 7.
[25] There is a very astute discussion of Struve's paintings in Ursula Schneider's afterword to *Spuren und Stürze*.
[26] *Spuren und Stürze*, p. 12.

Franz Boas,[27] who sent his students to study as many cultures as possible before these cultures disappeared, so Struve throughout his life traveled to remote places where nature was as yet undisturbed before they were invaded and overtaken by our modern technological civilization.[28] On our own continent he visited the Rockies, Yosemite, the parks in Washington and Alaska (not to mention the site of Thoreau's cabin). Into the 1970s Norway was an important destination.[29] He traveled the world round, going to places such as Nepal (where he dined across the street from the late king), Africa, New Zealand and islands in the Atlantic and to many other places. These travels served the encounter with the not of the world spoken of in "World and Reality."

In "Mysticism East and West and the Problem of Absolute Transcendence," Struve further explicates the distinction between the two types of transcendence and coins the terms "relative transcendence" and "absolute transcendence." After this lecture, he no longer uses these terms in print. They are so to speak nonce words that make a connection to convention, so that we might more clearly see what he is talking about. The theme of all three lectures could be said to be "absolute transcendence." He uses the distinction to make certain things clearer:

> And so the distinction between absolute and relative transcendence affords a sure criterion for differentiating philosophy and mysticism.
>
> A decisive insight—in fact it is the theme of my lecture—is that absolute transcendence is not merely an intensified relative transcendence, but a transcendence of a different kind. For not only the world, but also the ground of the world is transcended in absolute transcendence.

In this lecture he explores this distinction in historical texts from both the East and the West over the last two and a half thousand years. He says, "it is a one-sidedness of my presentation that I must completely leave aside Taoism and the fundamental problem of the relation to nature"; but he had already, in "World and Reality," discussed how the real as the not of the world is encountered in nature. For years Struve had been studying older Buddhism as we have it in the Pali Canon, and the fruits of this study are given us in the second and third lectures. Earlier he had intentionally left the contributions of the East "out of con-

---

[27] Franz Boas and Alfred Kroeber are generally considered to be the fathers of American anthropology. Margaret Mead and Zora Neale Hurston were two of Boas's more prominent students.

[28] See *Spuren und Stürze,* #126: "In spite of the general devastation of nature there are always still regions that it hasn't gotten to. You have to seek them out."

[29] Struve included some philosophical travel notes from Norway in *Der andere Zug* in a section called *"Bergtatt,"* a word he quotes from the Norwegian poet and mystic Sigbjørn Obstfelder, on whom he wrote an article (see bibliography). He says the word means literally "mountain taken," and is used in the sense of "enraptured," "ecstasy." Wittgenstein, too, was fascinated by Norway and periodically retreated there to a hut to work undisturbed.

sideration."[30] As his studies of Buddhism intensified, he no longer felt he could afford to do this. Heidegger had said that "a dialogue with the Greek thinkers and their language . . . still awaits its beginning. It is scarcely prepared for at all, and yet it itself remains for us the precondition of the inevitable dialogue with the East Asian world."[31] Struve countered that Nietzsche had decades before already begun this dialogue with his comments on Buddhism in *The Antichrist*. Struve is one of the initiators of this dialogue and continues it here. These studies led him to pay a visit to the German monk Nyanaponika, one of the pioneers of Buddhist studies in the West, in Sri Lanka during the course of his travels.[32]

It is the radical single-mindedness of older Buddhism that draws Struve to it; indeed it is in older Buddhism and in Meister Eckhart that he finds absolute transcendence most radically manifested. It is for this reason that he devotes so much space to older Buddhism and Meister Eckhart in both the second and the third lectures.

A paradox that Struve has called attention to over and over again is that I cannot go to the real; it must come to me. There is nothing I can do to bring about the real. I must wait patiently in readiness for it. The trains of thought in these lectures may be described as the preparation for its coming, that I may grasp the opportunity when the moment reveals it to me; I must be ready to make the leap:

> It must come over to me purely of its own accord: that is what is difficult and nearly unbearable about it.—If I try to go over to it of my own accord or to build a bridge to it or force some sort of flowing over, it will merely be imaginary . . .[33]

This is, as he says, no quietism; it must be done by me without my doing it. It can be readily understood that to read a true philosophical or mystical text requires that we not merely read the text with an eye to understanding how the one concept fits with the other, and so on, though such intellectual work is required, but that we be engaged with our whole person and allow a "complete inward presence of mind" to come up, a mindfulness of myself. Struve says in one of his aphorisms:

---

[30] See *Philosophie und Transzendenz: Eine Propädeutische Vorlesung* (Freiburg: Rombach, 1969), p. 21.
[31] "Science and Reflection" in *The Question Concerning Technology* translated by William Lovitt (New York: Harper & Row, 1977), p. 158.
[32] The Germans, going back to Arthur Schopenhauer, were perhaps the leading pioneers of Buddhist studies in the West, and many themselves became Buddhists. Some of the prominent German scholars were: Hermann Oldenberg, Karl Seidenstücker, Nyanatiloka and Nyanaponika, who was inspired by and joined Nyanatiloka at his Island Hermitage off the coast of Sri Lanka. The American monk and scholar Bhikkhu Bodhi studied with Nyanaponika.
[33] *Übergehn zur Wirklichkeit*, p. 75

Is my purpose knowledge? No; my purpose is relations to certain realities; and if knowledge, then only to the extent that it serves the establishment, strengthening and intensification of these relations.[34]

Struve viewed the third lecture, "On the Nonconformity of the Real," as in some ways the most radical and as forcing one to look beyond the surface *(der hintergründigste Vortrag)*. Indeed, by speaking of the *nonconformity* of the real, a new dimension comes into view in a way that it hadn't in the first two lectures, and the themes that will preoccupy him in the last decades of his life suggest themselves here. He no longer speaks of "absolute transcendence," or indeed even of transcendence. Not that he isn't still talking about what he had called "absolute transcendence," but here he is no longer interested in contrasting the two types of transcendence. The first two lectures had been published together under the title *Homo Mysticus*. This third lecture appeared by itself.[35] The way Struve attacks his theme makes itself felt while he is discussing a creation hymn from the *Rigveda*:

> What comes into view here is . . . that the real, reality in the ultimate sense, isn't merely inaccessible to knowledge and the understanding or that it transcends them, but that it is so to speak oppositional in form to them, and the nameless horror, which is inseparable from the recognition of this fact, becomes perceptible . . .

This is an entirely new tone, and confronting this horror becomes the dominant theme of this lecture. This experience is that the real does not conform to anything in the world or to my thoughts or to me. Struve brings testimonials to this experience from the West and East. "Nonconformity" is really a different concept from "otherness," though it so to speak includes otherness. But the "other" here is intensified to what does not conform in any way. What conforms has an underlying unity with what it conforms to. To become suddenly aware that the real does not conform to me evokes terror. We must face this terror and endure it "without lessening or mitigating it, until it unfolds its wholesomeness."[36] These are the terms Struve uses to describe the encounter with the real.

Struve brings his life-long interest in paintings to bear on this theme. Struve's own activity as a watercolor painter, already mentioned, indicates that he had a deep relation to the visual arts. Indeed, he had long appreciated the sense of nature displayed in Chinese paintings and in fact collected them. He had an especial interest in Max Beckmann and once stated that in the midst of all the horrible things during the National Socialist period and the War Beckmann buoyed the spirit by continuing to produce creative works of art. Since Beckmann was an "expressionist," he especially lends himself to the theme of

---

[34] *Übergehn zur Wirklichkeit*, p. 39
[35] He did have plans just before his death to republish (in German) "World and Reality" by itself and "Mysticism East and West and the Problem of Absolute Transcendence" and "On the Nonconformity of the Real" together.
[36] *See* below, p. 64.

the nonconformity of real through paintings which are obviously not naturalistic, and thus he became a target of the National Socialists, who branded them as "degenerate art."

Struve is concerned in this lecture to explore what reveals itself in a flash of insight as the nonconformity of the I and the "I think" of the understanding with the real. "The central thought of older Buddhism," Struve says, "is that the natural I-consciousness is illusory."[37] He explores this thought as it applies to Western thought as well, for, especially in philosophy since Descartes, the I has been a preoccupation of philosophy. Struve is interested in showing in the concluding portion of his lecture how all of what we accept as real is directly dependent upon the I-consciousness of the understanding, and thus is in a sense illusory. In order better to elucidate this Struve introduces the concept of *positing:* "What I have once posited in a wakeful state as real remains so for me, even if I refrain from it or forget it." P*ositing* here bears a relationship to the ὑποτίθεσθαι Plato speaks of in the *Phaedo*. Struve spoke of this in a paper at a conference in 1953 on "Experience and Metaphysics." There he says, "the *ideas* do not exist, or there are not ideas at all, but they only 'are' as 'hypotheses,' which . . . must be thought out and recollected anew over and over again . . ."[38] In short, we determine reality, which the *ideas* of Plato are, through just this positing, the *thesis* in *hypothesis*. But in Plato this *hypotithesthai* is thought of as a *raft*, which in fact Struve refers to in this third lecture, that is to say, as something to get us through.[39] Plato does not explicitly reflect on the positing of the I think of the understanding. Once the raft quality, that is, what we may call the provisional quality of this positing is left out of consideration, as it does in natural (non-philosophical) reflection, we start to find ourselves tangled in a net of illegitimate positings, for this is now not done *freely,* and freedom is the element of philosophy.[40] Now here is where Struve introduces something quite radical: he introduces as the opposite of *positing* the concept of *cancelling (tilgen):* just as only I can posit something as real for me, only I can cancel that positing. "Positing" is an act of spontaneity and thus has a binding character for me. When I "cancel" something I have posited, I have lifted this bond. "'Positing' and 'cancelling' show themselves thus to be ultimate intellectual and inner enactments."[41] These concepts take on a good deal of importance in his later philosophical notes.

In this context Struve speaks of *mindfulness,* as he had already in the second lecture, for as soon as I cease to be mindful, I will start to posit many things, for instance, all the ideas of the incessant dialogue society carries on with itself, as

---

[37] *See* below, p. 61.
[38] "Eine geschichtliche Erinnerung zum Thema: 'Erfahrung und Metaphysik,'" *Proceedings of the XIth International Congress of Philosophy*, Vol. IV, *Experience and Metaphysics* (1953), p. 131. This section of the conference was also attended by Etienne Gilson, Richard McKeon and Wilhelm Weischedel.
[39] *See* note 1 on p. 44 below.
[40] See Plato, *Sophist* 253c, which Struve referred to in lectures many times: η των ελευθέρων επιστήμη, "the free man's science."
[41] *See* p. 62 below.

real. "Mindfulness thereby proves itself to be the 'transcendental,' the highest virtue."[42] In this third lecture Struve adds a new concept: *trust*. How can the nonconformity of the real be endured? "For if the real cannot be measured by any measure, as is the case if it is that which does not conform, then my relation to it can only be that of naked trust."[43] In his later notes Struve will make a triad out of this, adding *gratitude:*

> Mindfulness; trust; gratitude.—Mindfulness sharpens the senses for the real; trust brings about the turn towards the real; gratitude makes possible the inflow of the real.[44]

As one looks at the course of these lectures one detects little changes in accent and vocabulary. And in this last lecture one can detect how Struve continues to develop a vocabulary adequate to the experience he wishes to articulate, as he has always found adequate words. What he says of the great philosophers also applies to him, as indeed it applies to anyone who has a genuine philosophical experience:

> Becoming older: distancing oneself from the origin; becoming younger: getting closer to it.—Spirit therefore is always becoming younger; nothing appears so youthful as the late works of the truly great ones.[45]

In closing, I would like to add a personal note. Wolfgang Struve was my teacher and doctoral advisor during my years at the University of Freiburg. I remember my first encounter with Struve was his seminar on Leibniz's *Monadology*. I was impressed by the precision and thoughtfulness with which he was able to think with and beyond Leibniz. I felt like Plotinus, who, upon hearing Ammonius in Alexandria, said to a friend, τοῦτον ἐζήτουν, "This was the man I was looking for."[46] It wasn't until a couple semesters later when I read my minutes of a seminar session on the second half of Kant's *Critique of Judgement*, and he became enthusiastic about my ability to follow Kant's train of thought, that he admitted me as a candidate for higher degrees.

The lecture courses were well attended. The foreign students in particular were attracted to his lectures by his staccato pronunciation, which rendered each word crystal clear, though it amused some of the German students a little. These courses were popular because they at once provided a general introduction to the philosophers under discussion and also penetrated deeply into the subject matter. It was characteristic of Struve that he could spice deep philosophical thoughts with humor: Struve often quoted Plato in his *Sixth Letter* saying that jesting was

---

[42] *See* p. 62 below.
[43] *See* p. 64 below.
[44] *Spuren und Stürze: Aufzeichnungen aus Skizzenbüchern 1984-1987*, #171.
[45] *Der andere Zug* (Salzburg-München: Stifterbibliothek, 1967/69), p.243.
[46] *Vita Plotini* 3.13, Porphyry's introduction to Plotinus, translated by Stephen MacKenna, Plotinus, *The Enneads* (London: Penguin, 1991—first published in 1917), p. civ.

the brother of seriousness.[47] In examining a concept, Struve would reveal for us all the thoughts contained in that concept, and this riveted our attention.

Over the years I attended a number of lecture courses and seminars on a wide range of philosophers from Heraclitus and Plato through Meister Eckhart and Descartes to Kant, Fichte, Kierkegaard and Nietzsche. In each case, Struve's own philosophical experience enabled him to see aspects of these philosophers that are often neglected. Thus these philosophers became for us living witnesses to philosophical thought and were not merely a matter of scholarship.

After completing my dissertation, I continued to maintain contact over the years. He never ceased to be an inspiration and friend to me. Struve died in the opening days of December 2011 at the age of 94. He has left us a treasure of writings which are both original and untimely ("untimely" in the sense of Nietzsche's use of the word in "Untimely Meditations"[48]). Thoughts are expressed in them that one does not encounter anywhere else. One of my fellow students, Till Beckmann, speaks of "these texts and their texture, which are of a rare fascination and attraction, which challenge us in a deep way and which certainly belong to the most precious in our time." Anyone who has an ear for these texts will discover this challenge and, by discovering it, will in some way meet it and in meeting it will have an encounter with the real.

*

When translating from one language into another, there are many instances when there would appear to be no exact equivalent for a word. Central to these lectures are the words *das Wirkliche* and *Wirklichkeit,* which, following custom, I have translated "the real" and "realtiy." But whereas *"wirken"* means to effect, bring about, produce, "real" comes from *res,* which means "thing," which would seem to imply something else.[49] But, fortunately for us, Struve justifies the traditional translation: "Today *Wirklichkeit* and *wirklich* very generally mean that which is. If we were to translate our *"Wirklicheit"* of today into Latin, we would render it neither with *actualitas* nor with *operabilitas,* but with *realitas.*"[50]

---

[47] 323 d.
[48] The first English translation of Nietzsche's *Unzeitgemäße Betrachtungen* was called *Thoughts Out of Season.*
[49] In *Philosophie und Transzendenz,* p. 180f., Struve quotes Hugo von Hofmannsthal in his *Buch der Freunde* (in *Aufzeichnungen,* 1959, p. 75): "That we Germans characterize what surrounds us as something that brings something about *[ein Wirkendes]* —die *'Wirklichkeit'*—the Latin Europeans as 'thingliness,' shows the fundamental difference of spirit and that they and we are at home in the world in entirely different ways."
[50] *Op. cit.,* p. 180.

Acknowledgements

There are several who have assisted in small ways and big ways in this work, and I would like to thank them here. In particular I would like to thank John Svitek, who made a thorough study of the text of "World and Reality" and made many suggestions. He also read through "On the Nonconformity of the Real" with me and made a few suggestions. I would also like to thank Mark Santos, who thoroughly read through "Mysticism East and West and the Problem of Absolute Transcendence" and made many suggestions. I have accepted almost all of their suggestions. Any blemishes that remain are mine. I have Till Beckmann to thank for the translation of the word *Vollzug* with "enactment," which I used immediately upon his response to my inquiry about this important term of Struve's because it reminded me of Stephen MacKenna's translation of Plotinus: "enacting the noblest life" for ζωήν τε ἀρίστην ἐνεργήσας. I have Professor Tom Nenon of the University of Memphis to thank for clarification of a couple tricky expressions. I would also like to thank Ursula Schneider for supplying me with the photograph of one of Struve's watercolors to put on the cover. Further, I would like to thank Professor Richard Polt of Xavier University, who took an interest in this project and located an appropriate publisher. Finally, I would like to thank the late Ralph Brave, who the very last time I spoke with him before his untimely death asked about the translation and put me in touch with Professor Polt.

World and Reality

Reflections on an Elementary Distinction in Philosophy

The topic of this lecture concerns thoughts which have occupied me for a long time, and the *Studium Generale* is certainly an excellent institution, not least of all because it gives a professor an opportunity to talk shop for once, not just to his students but to a larger audience.

Fichte says: "What sort of a philosophy one chooses depends on what sort of a man one is." Human beings cannot bring forth something other than what is in them; no two human beings are alike. Philosophy is therefore a unique thing and is obliged to be critical, not in the sense of claiming to know better, but in the sense of setting up boundaries between it and other things. As a product of finite human beings, philosophy can never be something which is finished and done with, but is something which is perpetually surpassing itself, just as humans do, so long as the spirit lives in them.

But the oft-quoted words of Fichte just now cited have a much larger and a much more fundamental meaning than may at first glance appear to be the case. I think, namely, that being human is something so unique and the mind something so finite that a particular philosophy cannot in the ultimate and strictest sense be communicated. Plato's *idea*, Kant's *reason*, Kierkegaard's *concept of existence*, Nietzsche's *thought of the eternal recurrence of the same* are at once such singular intellectual realities that, in truth, they were thought only once, could be thought only once, and that was by their authors. But for just this reason they are exemplary and an immense power and fascination emanates from them: that of the unfathomable core of the real.

What characterizes the thought about to be communicated here is the way in which the concept of transcendence will emerge and be intensified to the utmost. This is something that makes this thought a stranger in the present age, which could, generally speaking, be described by the phrase "loss of transcendence." The loss of the sense of genuine philosophical thought seems to me to be merely a consequence of this. Hence, a topic such as mine cannot today be dealt with in a straightforward manner, but requires an ongoing reflection on its method of treatment, and its justification. This has nothing to do with conveying a doctrine—I doubt whether the things which should be brought up here are even teachable—but only to awaken an understanding for certain ways of thinking. Perhaps then the stranger, in the sense of the Greek *Xénos*, could become a friend!

These reflections are, in part, difficult and abstract. Yet we are ultimately concerned with something quite simple, the difference between world and reality, and thus with sharpening our sense of this difference.

In the course of these reflections we will find that the deeper we penetrate into the matter, the greater will this difference become for us, and that means further that the doubts and resistance to this way of thinking which will arise in us will multiply, indeed will appear to be well-nigh insurmountable. This lies in the nature of our topic. After all, we belong to a world which asserts the identity of world and reality and seeks to prove it. We shall therefore have to encounter these charges continually. The experience of this inner resistance and the overcoming of it—this is what my lecture intends to talk about; it does not, however, purport to set up or develop a theory—be it a new one or an old one—of world and reality. That we cannot do so, and cannot be at peace with ourselves about our not being able to is just what we want to show.

World and reality are basic words in the vocabulary of modern man, both in his everyday speech as well as in that of literature and philosophy. Yet world sounds more familiar to us than reality, and less abstract. True, we speak of raw and hard reality and demand that we be realistic and down to earth, but, though there is a major German daily newspaper which calls itself "The World" and which doubtless claims to be especially close to reality, there is, after all, no newspaper called "Reality," and this title would also never develop the same attraction as the first. Indeed, world nowadays is a magical word, and carries everyone away in its spell. And this is so not only in politics, where one dare not omit it from any speech or article—even the newspaper just named claims to be "world renowned"—but just as much in all other areas of life. For instance, to go on a trip around the world seems to everybody something wonderful and good. Environment[1] is currently a catch-word that dare not be missing even from the back of a Nivea hand lotion tin.[2] And yet reality has no less importance in the vocabulary and everyday talk of today's man. Just take the formulaically fixed phrase: in reality: "In reality, it's not like that at all." Or consider the widespread use of the adverb "really," as in a question like: "Is it really true?" We sense the encompassing meaning of these words, but also the difference between them: in none of the examples given could we exchange the words. We sense this difference even where both words seem to mean the same thing in their most general collective sense, namely the quintessence of what is.

At this point we must make one of those comments on method which the treatment of our topic constantly demands. We would take world and reality in this entirely naive, general sense at first. We know that concepts like world and

---

[1] *Umwelt*—lit. "world around (us)." (Tr.)
[2] Nivea, a popular brand of hand lotion in the United States of America, is the most popular brand in Germany. (Tr.)

reality are not simply there, not simply available like stones, trees, houses and mountains, but are products of the human intellect which are developed over the course of a long philosophical tradition and which therefore presume along with all their gains also all their errors. We know that, aside from these historical reflections, analytical and positivistic reflection on language can come and seek to show that when we attach some sort of metaphysical meaning to such words, they are without object, deceptive and devoid of meaning. But we believe that the main thing is just to grasp and exhibit certain bodies of meaning that lie in our spirit and in our interior, not immediately to destroy the naïvety of our natural thinking through reflection, but indeed to lead it into its own all the more properly. For natural opining is characterized by its in a curious way becoming transposed and changing into its opposite as soon as it explicitly turns to metaphysical thoughts.

Now, a philosophical concept of world demands that we make the following as clear to ourselves as possible: to speak of the world qua world presupposes that we think and conceive along with it what is not world. For something can only become apparent by what it is not. We would like to call what is thought and conceived along with every understanding of the world what is other than world. And the question that is raised here is: What is that which is other than world? What is its relation to world?

Two great figures of thought may generally be distinguished within philosophy and outside as well, according to which this relationship and thereby the world itself is thought and apprehended, and it is about this that I would like to speak now.

According the first figure of thought, which is the predominate one, world and what is other than world are related to one another as that which arises from an origin and the origin itself; according to the second, which is more hidden, but not less operative and powerful, they are related to one another like illusion to reality.

The first figure of thought has taken on the most manifold forms and shapes within Western metaphysical thought. All metaphysics thinks according to this figure. Thus, for example, the Christian doctrine of creation: what is other than world is conceived of as God, and God as origin and creator; world is conceived as that which has arisen from the divine origin, and according to the doctrine of the *creatio continua*, continually and every moment arises from the origin. This same figure of thought forms the basis of the Neoplatonic metaphysics of emanation. What is other than world is conceived of as the transcendent primal one out of which the world has proceeded for all eternity, though not through a personal act of creation, but through an immanent outflow. As the intensity of experience and power of thought dwindles in late epochs, the origin as what is other than world can then get watered down to a vague idea of a universal reason or universal mind as the backdrop of all world events. The origin, conceived thus, gains that banal obviousness which reality has for us in familiar everyday things. In recent and most recent times, it has become popular to conceive world and what is other than world as two sides of one and the same reality, of which the one side is in its essence turned away from us. So, for example, the later Rilke in a famous letter to Witold Hulenwicz (of Nov. 13, 1925) writes: "Death is the side of life not shined upon and which is turned away from us . . . there is neither a here nor a beyond, but the great oneness, in which the beings that surpass us, the 'angels,' are at home." With this, Rilke gives expression to a typically modern sensibility, which is foreign to any duality. Rilke's strength didn't lie in abstract statements like this about his sense of existence. It is clear that if there is neither a here nor a beyond, there can also no longer be the great oneness Rilke speaks of, but the one disappears with the other, a consequence which Nietzsche had already drawn before Rilke.

If one thinks what is other than world as origin and the world as what arises out of that origin, then, no matter how one may conceive it in individual cases, the basic dialectic which characterizes any authentic relation to origin is: origin and what arises out of it must both be different from one another and be the same; they must be mutually dependent upon each other; and, finally, origin must possess a primacy over what arises out of it.

The more radically and decisively one thinks the relation to origin, the more sharply the elements of that dialectic come to the fore. The relation to origin is most radically experienced, however, in the philosophies tending towards mysticism. The great mystics—here I name above all Plotinus and Meister Eckhart—were therefore always also great dialecticians. The difference between origin and what arises from it in mysticism becomes otherness pure and simple: modern philosophy of religion still conceives God as the "wholly other"; the sameness of origin and what arises from it becomes identity: becoming one with God in the *unio mystica*.

It is important to note that the origin must also be dependent upon what arises from it, and not only what arises from origin dependent on origin. Thus we read in Angelus Silesius:

> I know that God can't live a moment without me,
> If I should perish, give up the ghost needs must he.

I quote this couplet here also because it is a model example of mystical utterance. Something quite abstract is expressed quite concretely; its expression is just as clear and simple as it is vivid and likely to be remembered. The shocking apparent anthropomorphism—he speaks having to give up the ghost, thus of God's having to die—serves, not only, through its paradoxicality, to call for reflection—after all, God is the immortal one—but renders the verses in a medium through which the unutterable authenticity of the statement shines through.—It is important that this aspect of the dialectics of origin not be left out, because it shows that the more radically one thinks the relation to origin, the more what arises out of it takes on a significance of its own and does not by any means diminish or even, as one might think, lose its significance. That means: the more radically I think the world as dependent on what is other than world, the more the world gains in significance.³

All philosophy, metaphysics and mysticism that thinks according to this figure conceives the world as having in some way fallen away from the origin or as having distanced itself from it, and the task becomes to reestablish the right relation to the origin, or just to gain this relationship in the first place.

Let us now place next to this general figure of thought a second great figure of thought, one which conceives the relation between world and what is other than world as that between illusion and reality.⁴ Historically, since the beginning of the philosophical thought of mankind, this figure of thought has been developed in the most diverse manner and form and has become a leading figure of thought, but it is deeper, more recondite, farther away from the superficial rationality of the everyday understanding. On the other hand, an elemental, all-pervasive basic feeling in man does correspond to it, which for the most part is suppressed and, where it breaks forth, all too easily fails to recognize itself. Misunderstandings suggest themselves easily enough, and suggest themselves in the closest thing of all, language. For language is fundamentally language of the world, that means, it has arisen so that we might make ourselves intelligible to one another within the world, not, however, to speak about the world. When it sets about doing so, it experiences a fundamental transformation: words take on the character of signs and symbols: they become "chiffres," sentences become ambiguous and full of meaning, their simple expression does not exhaust itself in the immediate, most proximate meaning but, shows beyond that what cannot be grasped with language, as for example the couplet by Angelus Silesius quoted just now. Early examples, one might say model examples of this are also the majority of Heraclitus's sayings.

Thus when we say that according to the second figure of thought the world is conceived and experienced as illusion, it is clear that illusion cannot be intended in a material or factual sense. For when we think world as illusion, we are thinking beyond all world, beyond all facts of the world; we have left the realm of the worldly. We will most readily appreciate this by taking illusion in its relationship to its opposite, reality, and in doing so we must surely be cognizant of the fact that this word likewise experiences the transformation we just spoke of. Illusion, seeming, in this most general sense means what is not real. Illusion needn't necessarily deceive. When we say that a work of art creates a beautiful illusion, we don't mean that there is something deceptive or misleading

---

³ In seminars, Struve pointed out how even Plotinus in the series of writings which conclude with his attack on the Gnostics defends the world, speaking of ο καλος ουτος κόσμος, "this beautiful world" (III.8.11.29). (Tr.)

⁴ Struve introduces this thought in *Übergehn zur Wirklichkeit: Philosophische und andere Reisenotizen* (Salzburg: Stifterbibliothek, 1970), p. 11f.: "I think about this and that, for instance, whether the mystic in moments of transport really lands at the origin of all these things or doesn't rather end up somewhere entirely different, at something which cannot be placed in *any* kind of relationship to world, and if in such a relationship, then not that of origin to what arises from origin, but instead that of reality to illusion . . ." (Tr.)

about it, but we also don't simply take illusion [German *Schein*, related to the English word "shine"] in the original sense of "brilliance," as the weakened forms preserved in such words as "sunshine" and "shine of the moon." Indeed, there is a certain element of deception, of illusion: what appears as real seduces us, so to speak, into taking it as real, even though it isn't real.

Therefore, for the second figure of thought, world is illusion in the sense that it proves to be not real vis-à-vis an other which is experienced and recognized as authentically real without its being placed in a relationship of origin and what arises from it. For otherwise we'd be back with the first figure of thought. We are not going to reflect on that here, and it is not necessary to do so here in order to get at what is peculiar to the first figure of thought. The world here loses any significance of its own, but by no means does it for that reason lose all meaning. Quite the contrary: it gains immense significance in a new sense, to the extent that it places itself before the real and sets itself the task of penetrating the illusion and of arriving at what is real, strictly speaking. An inhabitant of the world, inasmuch as he cannot leave the world forever, is only capable of this for moments, though he must employ all his time in attaining such moments.

He who has attained this, the "awakened one," "enlightened one,"[5] leads a double existence; he lives as it were side by side with the spheres of reality and world without vitally relating them to one another. The relationship of world and reality according to the second figure of thought is not a problem, or is only a pseudo-problem, because according to this figure no such relationship exists. Though according to this figure of thought the world as illusion does indeed obscure reality, reality is indifferent to illusion. The relationship of world and what is other than world, on the other hand, is *the* fundamental problem for the first figure of thought.

What is other than world in the second figure of thought has nothing to do with the world; what is other than world in the first figure of thought has everything to do with the world, inasmuch as the world of the first figure as that which has arisen from the origin is distinct from what is other than the world, but must dialectically once again be the same as it. One could say that what is other than world in the first figure of thought is something relatively transcendent—for transcendence requires every essential relationship to an origin—but what is other than world in the second figure is something absolutely transcendent, just as in general the difference between these two figures of thought lies in the conception and intensification of transcendence. The first one has a metaphysical and rational intention, the second a mystical and irrational intention. Seen historically and culturally, the first arises more from a Western, Christian sensibility, the second more from an Eastern, Buddhist sensibility. Yet it has appeared among us too, in mystical thought, for instance, in extreme passages in some of Meister Eckhart's sermons. One has often noted that there is a certain eastern element in all mysticism. For this reason, the mystics have always re-

---

[5] Struve has pointed out to me that the term "enlightened" depends on a Western conception of "light" which is foreign to the East. (Tr.)

mained outsiders among us in spite of an immense influence on philosophical thought. One primary example of this is Plotinus; and Meister Eckhart was brought to trial.

The more abstract a thought is, the more it needs to be rendered tangible to the senses, the more we need analogies appealing to the senses in order to understand it. It would be altogether wrong to think that an abstract thought couldn't bear them or that the rigor of thought would suffer losses. As a consequence of the finitude of rational thought, it needs such images and analogies more than ever. The great philosophers have known this. Just think of Plato's use of the Analogy of the Sun, the Analogy of the Line and the Allegory of the Cave in the middle of his *Republic* for the most abstract and least sensuous thing in his philosophy, the Idea of the Good, and the ascent to this highest idea. Casting about for images for these two figures of thought, we could, for instance, make the first figure tangible to ourselves with this image: Its other than world is like the sea, the shapeless and boundless sea, which washes around and comprehends the bounded, solid earth, a thing relating to shape and world. This earth has as it were come out of it and has taken its rise from it. No doubt the early Greeks had a similar sense of its arising, especially the first Western thinker we know of, Thales, who sets the tone for all subsequent thinkers: he thinks water—as the *apeiron*—as the origin of everything in general. The space which becomes tangible when shapes jut into it without touching it or being touched by it could serve as an image for what is other than world in the second figure of thought. Quite simply, that is above all else sensuously the mountains.

Here we have developed two possible ways of looking at the relation between world and what is other than world. Both are determinative for the basic metaphysical positions which human thought has formed in the most diverse modes; the second, however, is much rarer and much less sweeping. That is not surprising, for it is incomparably more difficult and sets higher demands, not only on speculative and dialectical thought, but generally on the entire inner strength of man. Today this figure of thought has to a large extent disintegrated and is becoming lost as a result of the increasing spread of the technological civilization of our age. One doesn't, for all that, comport oneself passively, but actively resists anything that demands such strength and seeks to expose its nullity. Strength has never yet been totalitarian—it has never needed to be—weakness always has been. The second position posits, to be sure, an absolute difference between world and reality. Modern man, generally in the habit of leveling everything down, finds such a position unbearable. People tend to characterize such a position as dualism: not a particularly felicitous coinage, carrying beyond that a certain evaluative accent, and people are quick to find objections. We shall here briefly name and discuss two of the chief objections.

According to the second figure of thought, world and reality have nothing to do with one another. But can something entirely without relation be thought at all? Does not the statement: A and B are without relation contradict itself on purely formal grounds? For when I say this I am already positing a relationship between A and B—which is already outwardly apparent when I join them together into a sentence. But such formal-logical arguments accomplish little here. They only demonstrate that complete lack of relation cannot be thought, is incomprehensible, but not that there is no such thing. That means it demonstrates the finitude of rational thought, which as soon as it goes up against the absolute gets caught up in contradictions—"strands," as Kierkegaard puts it.

The other so to speak ethical and practical objection would be that the world, conceived as illusion, has been disempowered too much, even if illusion is taken in a transcendental sense, and that it loses its independent significance. What is a modern industrial society, which daily demonstrates the reality of the factual and through its technological accomplishments provides spectacular proofs of its arbitrary, self-bound power, to make of such propositions? But when we argue in this way we are not thinking philosophically but functionalistically, as we do today to a much greater extent than we are even generally aware in consequence of our increasing dependence on technical appliances in everyday life. Thinking philosophically means: opening oneself up to and exposing oneself to what is incomprehensible about reality. We may only do that, however, when we disregard everything else.

We would like to further clarify the present problem through the following reflection. If A and B are distinct from one another in the strict sense then they can neither be bound to the other nor enter into opposition to the other—for every opposition presupposes something in common: this belongs to the elements of dialectics—they can, however, very much exclude one another: where A is, B cannot be, and the other way around. Let us assume for the moment that there is something to which A as well as B can belong. This would only then be possible such that it belonged either to the one or the other, but could not belong to both at the same time, and it could only change its relationship by switching from one to the other without being able to take something over in the course of this change, not even itself. In this sense it was earlier said that one who reached authenticity according to the second figure of thought leads a double existence, which is nothing bad, but refers us deep into the indissoluble and in no way reconcilable contradiction of finite existence.

We have developed two great possibilities of thought for the relationship between world and what is other than world. For which should we decide? Is such a decision not at all necessary because both hold their own and need not in any way contradict one another? This seems to me to be the case. The second figure of thought does not necessarily exclude the first but, if one will, reinforces it, and the first figure of thought only becomes wrong if it claims totality for itself, that is, when it holds the origin of the world, correctly understood as what is other than world, already to be absolutely what is other than world and thereby takes it together with the world as reality *in toto*.

That this cannot be the case may be briefly demonstrated here by the following dialectical consideration. Reality in the strict absolute sense cannot be finite. For if it were finite it could be thought and annulled. Reality, however, is what cannot be thought and annulled, is that to which our thought and sense come and run up against when it seeks to comprehend and contain everything in general and perceives that it cannot do that, whereby this perception itself is again ineffable. World, on the other hand, as something complete within itself, is in its essence finite. For in whatever way one conceives the world, this concept always means a whole which is in itself complete and returns back upon itself.— Since according to the dialectical propositions advanced earlier, origin and what arises from origin must be identical with one another, reality itself, supposing origin to represent reality, would thus have to be finite. Therefore we must conclude that the origin of the world cannot be reality, so little as the world itself can be. (One might want to counter that according this dialectic of origin and what arises from it the origin of the world must in essence also be distinct from the world and thus not finite. This is accurate. Strictly speaking we would put it this way: the origin of the world must be both finite and not finite, reality, on the other hand, can only be not finite. Its "infinity" is different in kind from that of the origin of the world and has nothing in common with it. Therefore we do better to speak of nonfinitude here.)

Dialectical trains of thought like these have become foreign to us today, but no conceptual thinking directed to the absolute can do without them. When we no longer find ourselves capable of opening ourselves up to the absolute or even deliberately, so far as that is possible, closing ourselves off to it, then such trains of thought must appear empty and idle. What do they mean in the present case? That true speculative thought, that is to say, thought which transcends, not only raises itself above the world and reverts to its origin, but necessarily raises itself above this collectivity, the world and its origin. How now should we define this thing to which this thought raises itself, reality in the authentic and ultimate sense?

Earlier in our exposition of the two figures of thought we coined the phrase: other than world. The origin of the world according to this would only be something relatively other to the world; reality in the ultimate sense, on the other hand, would be that which is in general absolutely other. But this manner of speaking has something unfortunate about it and can only be preliminary. It also easily leads to fundamental misunderstandings. We say, for instance, the other side. An extraordinary novel by Alfred Kubin bears this title. But the absolutely other which we speak of here does not mean the other side of the world; we could only say that, as we briefly discussed, with certain reservations about the relatively other of the first figure of thought. Moreover, this mode of expression, *the* other, lures us in spite of ourselves to objectify it and to make it into a thing, and that means once again to make worldly what in no way can be objectified and taken into the world and into our own thought. It seems to me that one of the chief deficiencies of modern philosophy of religion is the way it operates with the concept of the "wholly other." Once this becomes a fixed and unquestioned concept, all is lost.

Yet, as inhabitants of the world, we can only define and think reality in terms of the world. Thus, only one possibility remains, if we want to think reality without making it worldly and once again falling into illusion, and that is to negate the world, to think reality as the not [*das Nicht*] of the world. And what is primary and authentic about the type of experience of reality we speak of here is then this too: it is none of these things . . .

This way of speaking, "the not," may well sound unusual and odd to many. And it should; but, for all that, it is, in my opinion, in no way a far-fetched or affected way of speaking. Looking at it linguistically, this use of "*nicht*" was quite usual [in German] in earlier times. Thus we can read, for instance, in the 1522 (1521) Basel printing of Tauler: "Das nicht an dem die sel ruw findet das ist blosse gottheyt" (292 rb). ["The not on which the soul finds peace is pure godhead."] Instead of '*das Nicht*' ["the not,"], we would say "*das Nichts*" ["nothing"]. Just so, we still find in Luther the noun "*nicht,*" which in the course of the 16th century (acc. to *Trubner's Deutsches Wörterbuch*) gets pushed aside entirely by "*nichts.*" Yet the "substantive power" of the word *Nicht* has preserved itself in a few phrases to this very day, such as in "*zunichte werden*" ["come to nothing"] or in the still commonly used phrase, *hier ist meines Bleibens nicht* [I shall not stay here].

The Greeks—Plato and Aristotle—called wonder, or astonishment, the first fundament of philosophy. Wonder—at what? At what they declare to be the everlasting and inexhaustible theme of philosophical thought: being. But being cannot be thought as being without at the same time thinking its opposite along with it. That, however, is not-being, or, as both the Greeks and later philosophical tradition put it, nothing. So the question of nothing necessarily becomes thematic along with the question of being, but in this way, that it is averted. For the fundamental question is just this one of being and not the one of nothing. This is exactly how it stood with the first Western thinker of being, Parmenides of Elea. We can also put it like this: since its inception, classical Western philosophy as a "philosophy of being" has been nihilistic, namely by standing its ground against nihilism. This is not meant here in an evaluative much less in a pejorative sense. On the contrary, being becomes all the more lustrous and robust and is all the more grasped in thought the more it sets itself apart from its background and underground, nothing.

But the not we speak of here negates not only being, but just as much the not-being or nothing belonging to it. And if indeed against the backdrop of nothing being is something essentially wondrous, then we are transported to what is absolutely wondrous when we take this incomparably stronger negation seriously. And if just talking about being and nothing faultlessly and without contradiction presents us with nearly insurmountable difficulties, the difficulties now become all the greater, because with this negation language forfeits entirely its natural and accustomed function. This is just what we are trying to get at with this talk of the not.

The not is not something in the nature of an object. But then neither are the being and nothing of classical, traditional philosophy objects; they are not to be thought of as a something which has the property of being being or nothing, though they are still something which can be grasped and articulated by philosophy. "The not," on the other hand, is not to be understood as a phrase designating something that we could bring to mind as a standing content of thought once we are collected enough and have sufficiently concentrated on it, but is more to be understood as instruction for an inner enactment which, if it occurs without fault, lets me run up against something that I can neither apprehend nor keep hold of nor myself think, whose essence, however, at the moment of running up against it, at the moment of collision, lights up like a bolt of lightning. I say inner enactment. Indeed, in other respects we also call negation a logical act or a logical operation. It will be incumbent upon us later to show that the negation which we speak of here is not an activity; on the contrary, its enactment only occurs in the suspension of all activity.

It lies in the nature of the matter, as it does in language, that we secretly take the not, which does away with being just as much as it does away with nothing, as being one and the same as nothing. However we may conceive nothing, whether as the opposite, or as "the other," or as the "veil" of being, in each case we are thinking it in an essential relation to being and to world. We can call this nothing a world-nothing, the not, on the other hand, the not of the world.

The world-nothing is absolutely dreadful. "Absolutely" means to say: so dreadful that no intellectual being could endure bringing it to mind purely and without some sort of protection in between. We cannot live here at all without metaphysical illusion. The not of the world, on the other hand, is not dreadful. The lighting up in the moment of collision like a flash of lightening which we spoke of earlier means, in fact, a sheltering, which is not of the nature of the world. Here not only the world but also the nothing which is inseparable from the world has been done away with.

We can make this clearer still through the following reflection. World, as complete in itself, is finite. What is finite is burdened with nothing, and not just outwardly by having borders in time and space and by the fact that it can be destroyed, but it has been, as it were, totally penetrated by nothing, is in itself null. The not of the world is thus as the not of everything finite the not of the null. And that means: the not of the world is not the indifferent other facing the world but what is infinitely higher than it, is by this dialectic necessarily, if we may put it this way, not something below the world but above the world. This seems to me to be an important thought and a fundamental insight that when we negate what is finite in its essence we don't arrive at what is less than or lower than what is finite, to nothing and the null in the banal sense that the word has in everyday speech, but to what is infinitely higher and more, because negation of the finite is always a double negation, thus an affirmation which is not itself finite and can only be expressed in this way. Seen this way, the not of the world is the not of the not.

Yet dialectical determinations like these leave us unsatisfied in the end: What now is this not? Or with such a question have we already deviated from what we are concerned with here? For the question: what is it? demands an answer in the form: it is such and such. The not, however, is not a such. For according to Spinoza's dictum: *Omnis determinatio est negatio,* no determination and no grasping of it in conceptual terms is possible without negation; the not as the not of the world and the not of nothing, however, negate every negation. It is for this reason incomprehensible in the most strict sense.

Reality, as the not of the world, is that which is absolutely incomprehensible.

It is hard, and today harder than ever, to become serious about a thesis like this. I don't mean affirming or denying it—that's easily and quickly done — but gaining an actual inward relation to it. For the real is for us in the first instance ordinarily the familiar and the banal of everyday reality. This is what has been posited by man. Posited taken here in an extremely broad sense which pertains not only to what has been made and produced by man but also what he has put at his disposal. And to expose oneself to what in no way derives from man has no doubt become hard even in an outward sense. Heisenberg said in his lecture, "The Physicist's Conception of Nature": "In our age, however, we live in a world which man has changed so completely that in every sphere—whether we deal with the tools of daily life, whether we eat food which has been prepared by machines, or whether we travel in a countryside radically changed by man—we are always meeting man-made creations . . ." (printed [under the title: "Das Naturbild der heutigen Physik"] in *Die Künste im technischen Zeitalter*, Munich 1954, p. 61).[6] In the course of this, those things that derive from man and that he has manufactured, brought to a high pitch by technology—and which rule and determine our lives down to the slightest detail—have taken on the illusion of reality in itself to such an extent that they can scarcely be evaded. In considering this, one should by no means confine oneself to the spectacular, modern technical "super things" such as hydrogen bombs or space ships, which also wield an incalculable power over the collective psyche, not least of all through the propaganda that is inseparable from it, but this power is at its greatest, I believe, in the little, indifferent things of everyday use. Who would want to doubt the reality of a tin can or a plastic bottle?

Nor would we want to. But what we question is that the real of these things is actually the real. For the real—so we maintain—is the absolutely incomprehensible.

We could argue—and this is no doubt the prevailing view today: Reality may well be incomprehensible at its core—what's that got to do with me? What is incomprehensible is closed off to me and inaccessible. I for my own part keep to what can be comprehended. I've got enough concrete tasks on this earth. Why should I be dealing with the incomprehensible? Whoever talks this way will always meet with approval. For one thing, this is once again functionalistic reflection and not philosophical thought. (We are not behaving intellectually any differently from how we do when we operate ticket validators at the train station. And with what joy we operate such machines!) For another thing, I cannot in this way evade the claim and the pull of the incomprehensible. For, compared with the comprehensible and what is finite, the incomprehensible is as what is not finite—as we demonstrated earlier—something essentially higher and more

---

[6] Werner Heisenberg, *The Physicist's Conception of Nature*, translated from the German by Arnold J. Pomerans (New York: Harcourt, Brace and Company, 1958), p. 23. (Tr.)

valuable. I cannot, therefore, as a finite being be indifferent to it. Kant says at the end of his *Groundwork of the Metaphysic of Morals* that "while we do not comprehend the practical unconditioned necessity of the moral imperative, we do comprehend its incomprehensibility," which "is all that can fairly be asked of a philosophy which presses forward in its principles to the very limit of human reason."[7] In other words, we can comprehend that we cannot comprehend here and therefore have nothing further to think about. But that is not how it is with what is absolutely incomprehensible, in other words, reality. We can draw no borders here in the area Kant is concerned with; we cannot settle down and assert ourselves in the face of the incomprehensible. There is so to speak no safe haven, not even an inner one, into which I could withdraw and take shelter from it.

The incomprehensible is not, in fact, graspable by the understanding. But that does not in any way mean that all conceptual thought has to come to a halt in its presence. On the contrary, this thinking experiences its utmost intensification by means of it. We cannot grasp it in thought, but we can run up against it in thought. To do this, we will simply have to think.

Yet such thought is not enough by itself. If it is to be more than a mere intellectual operation, then the real must be bodily experienced before any act of thought. How otherwise is thought to run up against it?

Where and how is the real experienced as the not of the world?

To start with, the answer must be quite simple: In nature—just as the experience of nature is decisive for every experience of reality one has—but this general answer now requires definition and development. That is to say, nature has two essentially different aspects, a worldly and a magical side, if you will.

To the first, the worldly aspect of nature: When on beautiful days, say, on a splendid summer day, nature lies there as if celebrating in the light of the sun, it seems to be doing only one thing: confirming human beings in their earthly existence who then no doubt gratefully praise "this green earth" and "this beautiful world," feel secure in nature and utter their yes! to it. But they cannot hide from themselves—and least of all modern humans—that this security is only relative and temporary, indeed, in truth only apparently offers security. We know today: Earth will one day be destroyed in a frightful cosmic catastrophe and be taken back into the sun as it burns out. Neither does it lie in the lap and center of the universe but lies "somewhere" in a "corner" (Pascal)[8] of cosmic nature within

---

[7] *The Moral Law: Groundwork of the Metaphysic of Morals*. Translated by H. J. Paton (London and New York: Routledge, 1991; first published by Hutchinson in 1948), p. 148. (Tr.)

[8] Struve refers in *Philosophie und Transzendenz: Eine Propädeutische Vorlesung* (Freiburg: Rombach, 1969), p.111, to Blaise Pascal's *Pensées* #194, translated in *Pascal's Pensées* (introd. to the reprint by T. S. Eliot: no translator given—New York: Dutton & Co., 1958; orig. Everyman ed. 1911) , p. 55 "I see those frightful spaces of the universe which surround me, and I find myself tied to one corner of this vast expanse, without knowing why I am put in this place rather than in another, nor why the short time which is given me to live is assigned to me at this point rather than at another of the whole eter-

the totality of which it represents something like an incidental niche for organic life, whereby its production can hardly any longer be viewed as the goal of the cosmic process; indeed, organic life comes across as an outsider in it. Nevertheless, we don't need to go so far into the cosmic dimension to become aware that nature is always also what is foreign to us, "unrelated" (Rilke), indeed, is properly speaking this, as soon as we engage ourselves more closely with it. Anyone who has lain in the grass on such a summer day and immersed himself in his immediate surroundings with an attitude of tender regard, such as Dürer in his portrayal of a blade of grass, or Gessner in his not less masterly description in *Contemplations Among the Grass*[9] have done—when he suddenly observes ants clinging to the wings of a dragonfly while other ants bite out its eyes in order to render it defenseless—will sense how here below the beautiful illusion there lurks a nameless dread.

Then, too, nature can point to something which it is not and which does not come out of its substance but is completely different from it, is not in it, but with respect to it: to the real as the incomprehensible not of nature. Then nature becomes magical. But this magical quality is not to be confused with that foreignness and that dread we just spoke of, which are in nature itself and which essentially belong to its primal matter.

In the first case, nature is seen and experienced as "material" in the best and deepest sense of the word. Nature brought forth humankind out of itself and is its "womb," yet nature is something less than mankind, mankind having by its own devices raised itself up out of nature, as what is unconscious, to the light of consciousness: nature is, as it were, the necessary, yet subhuman substratum of mankind's human existence. In the second case, nature is experienced as the placeholder of the real, which transcends nature entirely—nature as that which brings me to the real and transports me there.

Two very distinct "functions" of nature, which have nothing as such to do with each other, but which we do not keep apart most of the time. The one side and conception of nature leads, among other things, to modern science and technology, the other to mysticism and religion.

Though both aspects of nature are indeed very different, they in no way exclude one another. The pernicious thing in all this is that nature ceases to be a placeholder as soon as it is no longer left undisturbed by itself, as soon as humans view it chiefly or even solely as matter, now taken in the banal sense as

---

nity which was before me or which shall come after me. I see nothing but infinities on all sides, which surround me as an atom, and as a shadow which endures only for an instant and returns no more." Commenting on this passage, Struve says, "and here the finitude of human beings finds its sharpest expression; they are as spatial beings finite because they do not know why they have been set in precisely this place and no other. In French the word is *'placé.'* Modern existential philosophy will then later step it up a notch and speak of the 'thrownness' of man." (Tr.)

[9] *Die Gegend im Gras* by Salomon Gessner in his *Idyllen* (1756 and 1772). Salomon Gessner (1730 - 1788) was Swiss painter and poet. A translation (under the title cited in the text) appeared in *The Works of Solomon Gessner* (1805). (Tr.)

material to be worked over, as the object of a technologically driven science of nature and of the technological domination and use of nature, which results from it. By the way, if the magical power of nature to refer me to the real is to become operative, then nature must not only be left untouched and undisturbed, but I must myself also be directly exposed to it without any artifices and without any articficial enclosures. For this reason, for instance, a sojourn on the moon would accomplish nothing in this regard.

Today people have begun—for some time now—beyond even all rational consideration, I believe, to suspect what it means that the net of technological contrivances is becoming even denser and soon will have covered every last spot on our terrestrial globe, or rather already has. This has become an irreversible process, and people attempt to check this process and, as it were, save what still can be saved, for example, through the establishment of national parks. In this respect, they are quite radical in the United States of America: visitors in national parks are not allowed even to pick up a stone lying on a footpath and set it down somewhere else, let alone put it in their pockets and carry it off! But even the meticulously rigorous observance of such rules cannot as yet teach us to perceive nature purely as such; for when I have declared an area to be a nature preserve, it has already become an object of human use, moreover, a source of national pride as well. ("Nature preserve" seems altogether a questionable coinage. It should be called rather a "human being preserve." We don't want to protect nature for its own sake, even where parks are closed off to tourism, but rather to protect humankind from the destruction of nature which it has set in motion, thus really to protect humans from themselves.)

I come now to the second question: How is the real experienced as the not of the world? The not of the world as the absolutely incomprehensible and as the non-finite is that which does not in any way derive from me. That means it can only reach and affect me if at the moment it touches me I am not active in any way.

We can also make this clear to ourselves by means of the following reflection: All experiencing in the world is an active apprehension of an object, is always, as Kant has shown in his transcendental-philosophical discussions, at once receptivity and spontaneity. Not so the experiencing of what has not got the character of world. We cannot for this reason say, for instance, it is pure receptivity without spontaneity. There is no such thing. Rather, we must recognize that these categories do not apply here, that the experience of what is not world and not an I must be of an entirely different form.

The not of the world is experienced by my suspending all activity.

As is well known, the Greeks have shown leisure to be the basic condition for any philosophizing. Philosophy can then, and only then, come into being when the immediate needs of life have been satisfied and there is nothing immediately pressing in our lives. Meanwhile, suspension of all activity is more than and different from leisure. We are capable of it only for moments, just as we can only suspend breathing for moments: it demands, as it were, a stopping of the natural drive of life. That is hard. Suspension of all activity is not itself an activity—where it is that, one is only seemingly suspending activity—but, all the same, it must be practiced. Practice taken in the essential sense, as we do here, means: coming back to the same thing over and over again.

Suspension of all activity thus does not mean quietism, passivity, indolence; it is, rather, action in an eminent and pregnant sense: for nothing so completely changes our existing situation as this.

As a consequence of this: There is no action having a higher value. That must be said clearly and unambiguously, even though everything in mankind in its natural state and even more in modern mankind, thus everything in us, resists a proposition like this at first. For we know action chiefly as acting and reacting, which the bustle of modern life incessantly demands if a person is trying to escape being run over; and this would scarcely change in spite of the automobile-free pedestrian zones, which in recent times large cities have been setting up in their centers. Whoever acts and reacts—and really only does the latter—is, of course, merely a "product of his environment": for even if he wishes to change his environment, he has been determined by it, that is, by its respective state, which he wishes to transform into a different one, and he has been determined by his very desire, which has been provoked by this state of the world and by the will which it has called forth; thus he is not free. One acts in order to achieve something in the world; one reacts in order to deal with the attacks from the world. Action in the eminent sense is, however, neither the one nor the other, but detaching oneself from the world.

Detachment from the world does not mean resignation. Resignation means that one has abandoned action. One can only act when one has found one's way back to that point of one's being from which one is totally free, and which is also the source point of all primordial metaphysical conviction. In order to attain this, a kind of stillness is needed, which means the falling away of world. Only in this way can one recognize the false actions and reactions which for the most part make up our entire doing, inner as well as outer. But recognizing this is already overcoming it.

Detachment from the world in this sense does not, for instance, mean to be without a relation to the world: that is something we can never do as human beings, and beyond that it would be a foolish demand; but it does mean to clarify our relation to the world until nothing having the character of world that could bind us is there any longer.

Action in the eminent sense is therefore always highly moral. For "moral" means that something obligates us unconditionally. Since everything worldly is conditioned, such an obligation can only proceed from what is not worldly. What is highly moral, moreover, obligates unconditionally to such a degree that we do not recognize it as a value, but, though we do not blindly accede to its demand, we do so without any reflection.

World and reality: Up to now we've been proceeding methodologically in such a way that we have been taking both these basic concepts, as philosophical concepts, simply as given, and have been operating with them naïvely. In the last part of the lecture we must put this naïvety in question. Admittedly not in the sense that we doubt whether these terms might be without meaning and content, and thus merely deceptive. That this procedure would be far more uncritical than the first, my elucidations for their part—so I hope at least—have made clear—and I often wonder that modern critics of philosophy are not more critical of their own critical consciousness. Often they are like the man carrying a sign through the streets of New York on which he had written in large letters: "Away with all signs!" But now we must accommodate the desires and the unrest of our philosophical impulse, and also the enigmatic depth of metaphysical thought, with a question, through which all propositions advanced up to now will experience an encompassing transformation and will no longer remain unmediated assertions, but will become something akin to "hypotheses" in the Platonic sense, that is, they will become "springboards" to something else. This question, through which we shall reach a frame of mind wholly different from the earlier frame of mind, if we are successful in confronting it, is: Where do we stand, properly speaking, when we talk about world and reality?

To speak this way presupposes that we can distance ourselves from both world and reality and can somehow place ourselves outside them. That we can distance ourselves from the world—this may still perhaps be possible in isolated extraordinary moments in which we, as it were, swing ourselves beyond world and life; but how are we to distance ourselves from reality, which again and again overcomes every distance and takes it back into itself? Furthermore: the little word "and," as a conjunction, links both. But such a linkage presupposes something again encompassing world and reality, a "metareality," so to speak, and a "metaspace" they are in. I take a malicious pleasure in seeing how easily and carelessly present-day reflection by philosophy of science, which prides itself not a little on its progressive intellectual stance and believes it has long since left all metaphysics behind, "tries to get behind" the appearances of things by using word-formations with *meta*, such as *metacritique, metatheory, metapsychology*. I've even run across *metaphilosophy*. But to say that there is no world behind the world and no theory behind theory—does not end philosophical thought; but it is by making this clear to oneself, and not only by thoroughly making it clear, but by experiencing this clarity with every fiber of one's intellect, that philosophical thought first begins.

With the question, where then do we stand, who ponder and speak about world and reality, as if there were, at bottom, nothing at all particularly special about it, we enter an abyss, and perhaps for moments we enter so far into this abyss that we can no longer take our stand on the ground of a presumed metareality, which we admittedly do naturally and must do in order to be able to exist at all as intellectual finite beings. For in the medium of our everyday intellectual life we are subject to bias and held captive to the illusion of reality presented by the banality of the world. Seen metaphysically, we are damned to lie. Not only do we lie into existence what doesn't exist; worse still, we generally have to lie out of existence what truly is: the real.

We tumble into something bottomless, or rather: the bottomless, because it cannot really be without bottom, reveals the metaphysically superficial, deceptive and illusory in all human finite thought, thus in all thought as such. For this finitude does not come from an insufficient expansion and development of our intellect, but rather from the inner form of thought as such. It can only be experienced by thinking, by setting one's thought in motion, but without one's being able to think and express or divulge this experience itself, directly or indirectly. Wittgenstein closes his *Tractatus Logico-Philosophicus* with a proposition of enormous suggestive appeal, finding adherents: "What we cannot speak about we must pass over in silence."[10] But we cannot also say that we must pass over in silence what we must be absolutely silent about; we can only show by our speaking that we must.

Metaphysical unrest, which is not finite, cannot be taken away or assuaged by thought, which is in itself finite. It will only then be assuaged when one is engaging with the real. But then one won't be thinking and speaking any more. Engaging with something means neither being in it nor away from it, which in the case of the real is not possible. But one does not arrive at the real without previously having spoken and thought. Engaging with the real is not something temporal, and that means: seen from the perspective of time it is something momentary. The moment does not last, neither briefly nor for a long time.

Metaphysical unrest—what is it really? Nothing other than the infinitely assailing and tensing of the incomprehensible pull of the real, or more precisely, usually the absence of this pull, in special moments and hours, of this pull itself. Infinitely assailing is the being, infinitely tensing is the doing of him who exposes himself to it.

The life of the world that we naturally and normally lead and must lead, only becomes possible by ignoring this gnawing unrest, and that means either giving ourselves over to resignation metaphysically or deciding for illusion. The reverse side of this tends to be an intensified activity, which consumes itself. If, on the other hand, we accommodate this unrest and its infinite demand, it can happen that an incredible sudden change or reversal takes place, which in no respect originates with ourselves, cannot be made or brought about by us and for just this reason must seem in the strictest sense unbelievable: that we no longer generate the stuff of ourselves and posit world and rely on what is our own, but reality comes over one and takes us over to it, and in a literal sense, receives us.

If this takes place, then the sudden change also takes place that one no longer experiences tumbling into a bottomless abyss as something bad and "negative," but as *the* inner liberation and release that matters. For one recognizes that there isn't and can't be any bottom or base of any sort whatsoever. If one really sees this, then, too, one cannot now set oneself on the base of the knowledge that there is no bottom or base, rather one becomes aware that settling down on an ultimate base, though indeed necessary for an intellectual being having the char-

---

[10] Translated by David F. Pears and Brian F. McGuinness (Oxford: Routledge, 1961), G. E. Moore came up with the Latin title for the 1922 edition of the German text with a translation by F. P. Ramsey and C. K. Ogden in allusion to Spinoza's *Tractatus Theologico-Politicus*. (Tr.)

acter of an I to be able to assert itself in the world, this being can transform this necessity once again in an ultimate and singular sense into freedom.

Kant says in the "Transcendental Dialectic" of his *Critique of Pure Reason* that "transcendental illusion" is an illusion that cannot be avoided. Transcendental criticism can indeed unveil this illusion and in so doing prevent us from being deceived by it, but it cannot make it disappear, just as the stick held in water appears bent, even though I know that this is a consequence of light refraction; but when I recognize this, I will no longer be deceived by this illusion.

This situation is even more full of pitfalls with the illusion of an ultimate ground, the ground of the comprehensible, from which viewpoint even Kant makes his arguments and must, in as much as he takes a metaphysical position and takes his stand in the thinking I and develops a philosophical system as a rational edifice of doctrine. Not only does the illusion remain after I have seen through it, but I must keep on letting myself be deceived by it if I wish to assert myself in the finite world as an intellectual being having the character of an I. To remain in the metaphor: I must keep on believing against my better judgement that the stick is bent. Only by seeing through the illusion and continuing to believe that it is bent do I arrive at the real and thus at a freedom which is not mere finite illusion.

Philosophical thought, which is worldly thought, can lead up to this, but no further. Beyond this is no longer philosophy, no longer intellect, no longer community, no longer awareness, no longer security. Instead, there is a depth of reality which is unfathomable and unfathomably pulls and shelters us . . .

What has been said in this lecture? I have always believed that if something has been said at all in a lecture it must be possible to express it in a sentence. What has been said is: World and reality have nothing to do with one another. But having nothing at all to do with one another—that is a strange and remarkable thing.

What I have nothing to do with at all, I do not accept, nor I do reject it, nor am I indifferent to it. For in each case I am positing a relation.

But total lack of relation is incomprehensible. Reality is incomprehensibility. If I am serious about my having nothing to do with anything, then, for me, the matter in question moves into the incomprehensible, and that means into the real, in the sharpest sense. Thus, if I become serious about the metaphysical illusion of the world, then the world doesn't for that reason fall away, but for the first time moves into the real.

The world and the things of the world become real in a different, entirely new way: not in an objective way, not in a functional way, not in the sense of some dull, worldly faith, but in an unprecedented way which is both more and less.

For the age in which we find ourselves it seems high time that the world and time become real in this way, if it wishes to endure.

Mysticism East and West and the Problem of Absolute Transcendence

The words and concepts that make up the theme of my lecture are conventional, abstract, loaded down with tradition, artificial and other worldly: in short, they are unbearable and enough to drive one away. But you are here, and I would like to try and foster an understanding for a problem that seems to me to be of far-reaching importance and topical as well.

The subject of my lecture is as simple as it is difficult and intricate. It cannot be otherwise, if it is to be true. It is not conventional: not only in the sense that it does not conform to the dominant conventions, but in the sense that it cannot be conceived at all by the conventional means of speech and thought.

Yet we cannot make the unconventional intelligible to ourselves unless we take convention as our starting point—and our task then will be to get from what is conventional to what is unconventional. Some sort of an inward readiness will be needed for that. What is unconventional is by its very nature indifferent to convention: the converse is, however, not the case. We struggle resolutely against what appears strange to us and lies outside the purview of the familiar. And the difficulties are increased not so much by their involving rational comprehension as by their requiring us to overcome basic inner tendencies which characterize our age. As I go along I shall call attention to those points in my lecture where this basic resistance becomes especially great.

Every kind of thought requires not only intellectual ability, but also moral qualities. These last, as will be seen later, are required in a very special sense for a kind of thinking belonging to mysticism.

It is conventional to speak of "*west-östliche Mystik*." A well-known book by Rudolf Otto bears this title, the expression no doubt originating with Goethe's *West-östliches Divan*, or *Divan of the West and East*. Certainly it should have been "*Öst-westlich*"—only that sounds too odd to us.[1] It would appear that mysticism has its origin in the East and appeals more to the Asian than to the European. In Greek civilization it was, to borrow a well-known phrase from Erwin Rohde, a drop of foreign blood, and this it has remained for Western man ever since. To divide and oppose East and West is to simplify matters much too much and to stereotype, an opposition which in politics—and not only in politics—for many more or less amounts to the opposition between good and evil.

As is well-known, it was not until late, not until the last century, that the West began to occupy itself seriously with Eastern civilization. Today, now that mankind has long since been joined into one by modern means of communication and transportation, we can no longer neglect the East in our studies, nor may we feign ignorance; moreover, modern scholarship provides us with tools such that, even if we do not happen to be specialists, we can study the East with due thoroughness and care.

We are not interested in playing off the East against the West, but, so to speak, in getting "beyond good and evil" to what we would—once again conventionally—call absolute transcendence.—Both components of this expression come from post-classical Latin. We would employ them heuristically only. They could be translated into English as: "climbing beyond, pure and simple."—It is clear what we are to transcend: transcendence has since time immemorial stood in relation to the world—"world" understood as the sum of absolutely everything there is.

We may speak of absolute transcendence only in comparison with and in distinction from relative transcendence. By "relative transcendence" I understand passing beyond the world to its origin. This kind of passing beyond occurs in all philosophical thought, nay, it is its essence. Since its inception, that is, since the Greeks, since Plato and Aristotle and those still more ancient, philosophy has been the "science of first causes." Philosophical thought is therefore in its essence metaphysical in the broadest sense of the word. Even Kant's transcendental and critical thought is such.

All metaphysical thought transcends the world—not to leave it, but to lay hold of it at last at its foundation. All passing beyond the world in philosophical thought, when it occurs in the dimension of cause, remains relative to the world. That is the greatness, but also the—very definite—boundary of philosophical reflection.

Absolute transcendence, on the other hand, means passing beyond the world so as to leave it and not come back to it again. Mysticism strictly so-called has to do with this type of transcendence only, just as philosophy has to do with relative transcendence only. And so the distinction between absolute and relative transcendence affords a sure criterion for differentiating philosophy and mysticism.

---

[1] English speakers are free, however, to restore the word order to "east and west," which sounds more natural in English, and Rudolf Otto's book *West-östliche Mystik* was in fact translated into English as *Mysticism East and West*, which no doubt indicated a feeling on the part of the translator that "East" at least sounds better first in English. (Tr.)

A decisive insight—in fact it is the theme of my lecture—is that absolute transcendence is not merely an intensified relative transcendence, but a transcendence of a different kind. For not only the world, but also the ground of the world is transcended in absolute transcendence.

Here is one point where resistance makes itself felt: something, indeed, everything in us struggles against this type of transcendence. Why that? What does it mean? Can anything of the kind even be thought?

Can it be thought? Yes and no. It must be thought, but it cannot be thought.—It must be thought in as much as my thought cannot stand still anywhere but is compelled by its very nature and by the nature of intellectuality, when it thinks something, to think at the same time—expressly or implicitly—of that which is not what it thinks. When I think of the world and its ground I must also think of what they are not; together with them I must think of what is absolutely different from them. It is unthinkable to the extent that absolute otherness is unthinkable. For thinking is the setting up of relations. And the thought of absolute otherness does away with all relation.

These last remarks will seem paradoxical and vexing. But it does not by any means follow from something's being inaccessible to thought, from its being logically incomprehensible, that there is no such thing. Leaving something completely behind, that is, not referring myself back to it in any way, is something that can only be performed or done: it is not something that can be thought. To give the example of examples: it is neither conceivable nor thinkable how I should be able to leave myself completely behind.

It will be apparent that the absolute in the sense in which we have been speaking of it has nothing to do with the "absolute" of German idealism. No matter how much German idealism intensifies the idea of the absolute and no matter how much territory the absolute is conceived to comprehend, no matter whether as that which comprehends the correlation of subject and object, as that which comprehends identity and difference, or as the identity of identity and difference, or in some other way, German idealism essentially stays within the domain of logical and dialectical thought. For German idealism is philosophy, not mysticism, and will never be anything else: it is in a relationship to the world.—Nietzsche has his Zarathustra say in "The Drunken Song": "The world is deep . . .";[2] but absolute transcendence is no depth of world.

As for the expression "mysticism," now an established term, it is not without a certain charm, but neither does it lack its defects, as is generally the case with such words. Even the right definition and derivation of the word "mysticism" is a matter of dispute; and I shall forgo adding to the countless more of less profound explanations of the word yet another. Little would be gained by any new addition to the list. But it can indeed be said that there are certain texts, such as Plotinus's writings and Eckhart's and Tauler's sermons, which are clearly mystical in kind, and which differ from non-mystical texts not only as a whole, but in every sentence and word. If one has an ear for what is mystical,

---

[2] *Thus Spoke Zarathustra: A Book for All and None*, translated by Walter Kaufman (New York: The Viking Press, 1954), p. 320. (Tr.)

one recognizes them immediately. They are touchstones of themselves, and for just this reason can't be defined by something external to themselves, by something other than themselves.

Moreover, mysticism, in the general estimation of its thoughtful students, is a kind of ferment that has proved fruitful for philosophical no less than for religious thought, up to a point; beyond that point, however, its influence is looked upon as and felt to be destructive and harmful, the reason being that all philosophy and every institutionalized religion is concerned with the world, whereas mysticism, by its inmost intention, aims at leaving the world, never to return. This the world does its utmost to oppose.[3]—And to me this seems to be one of the underlying reasons why the Church put Meister Eckhart on trial, and had to, and why Plotinus, despite his immense influence and despite the number of those who study him, has remained a stranger to classical philology and philosophy.

Philosophy is "wisdom of the world," religion, as institutionalized religion, is "world-religion"; but there is no such thing as "world-mysticism." Rather, mysticism has to do with what is not world.

A second and related point is that we are used to having to make an effort to achieve something we want. Indeed, this expectation has so much become second nature to us as members of modern industrial society that we no longer either know or are able to conceive of things' being otherwise.

Now it is clear that what I can achieve by making an effort, and what everyone together can achieve by making an effort, can only be something relative and finite and limited. Therefore, in the realm of absolute transcendence such behavior is out of the question. Instead, I must first of all and above all free myself completely from the prejudice that I could do something there by my own efforts. It isn't easy. Indeed, it calls for the tedious process of a complete inward re-orientation, and nowhere is there so much self-deception and self-delusion as here.

Furthermore, our age is marked by an inclination restlessly to call to mind all and sundry, and is served in doing so to a large extent by the means of modern technology. Absolute transcendence, on the other hand, cannot be called to mind. If I try to call it to mind by thinking, by straining my will, or by whatever

---

[3] See *Wir und Es* (Zürich: Max Niehans, 1957), p. 58f.:
"Levels of Action.
    "First Level:
        "Doing and bringing about. We can always do it. As "work" sanctioned by modern society. The worker.—Industry, diligence, action, success.
    "Second Level:
        "Renouncing doing and producing. Creating. We can only occasionally do it. Tolerated by Society. The artist and the philosopher.—Leisure, favor, production, work of art or philosophy.
    "Third Level:
        "Renouncing even producing. Alteration of the whole. We can't do it at all. Outside the purview of society. The prophet and the saint.—Detachment, grace, inspiration, deed." (Tr.)

means, I shall fail, and the harder I exert myself, the worse I shall fail. It must instead present itself to me. Moreover, the way in which it presents itself differs in kind from our own way of calling things to mind: it presents itself through a simple act of self-announcement and self-legitimation. An act on our part of taking in or of accepting what is presented by means of organs is not involved. Again, I must not yield to the natural urge to grasp and hold on to what announces itself in this way, not even by means of language. If I attempt to do so, it will elude me once again. Rather, I must for my part keep perfectly still. This is not a prescription for "quietism." What matters I must do for myself, no one else can do it for me. But I must do what matters without doing it; that is, I must not do it with my own powers and capacities. It follows from this alone that redemption by one's own efforts is no less nonsense, the way mysticism sees things, than is redemption through some foreign agency.

This inward re-orientation, for no one so difficult and for no one as less likely than for present-day man, is not yet meditation but is the indispensable prerequisite of meditation. This fact is a measure of the value, all in all, of what is offered under the exalted title of "meditation" nowadays.—Perhaps it was Descartes who set in motion the process that has perverted the term and emptied it of meaning. Anyhow, it seems ironic that he should have given the title "Meditationes" to that writing of his which gave expression to and is paradigmatic of our modern European self-assurance, an attitude that has once and for all excluded meditation in the sense adumbrated.

Now, to amplify what I mean by absolute transcendence, I would like to speak about a few basic doctrines from older Buddhism and then call some mystical texts into evidence. The chief non-Christian mystic will be Plotinus, the chief Christian witnesses, Dionysius Areopagita and Meister Eckhart. It is clear that when one has a gigantic area of study before one, one can only present a little bit, and even that only in a very much abbreviated form. Beyond that, it is a one-sidedness of my presentation that I must completely leave aside Taoism and the fundamental problem of the relation to nature—which is indeed to be distinguished from the technological problem of damage done to the environment.

That older Buddhism—the name "Buddhism" is by the way European in origin—, Hinayana Buddhism (the more recent, Mahayana Buddhism will be discussed only by way of contrast) is unique in the spiritual history of mankind is a fact that has often been pointed out and that seems the more remarkable since, as historians of religion are in growing numbers recognizing, older Buddhism is in many respects not at all original as compared with other contemporary religions, such as Jainism. I would now like to discuss three basic thoughts of older Buddhism:

1. The doctrine of not-I *(anatta)*
2. The rejection of all metaphysical assertions and judgements
3. The concept of *nirvâna*

Our task here is to see how each thought is inseparably tied to the others. Each demands the others. None can be altered without the others also being altered. In the course of this lecture I shall be presenting three steps in thought, which are three levels of consideration.

One might ask whether Buddhism has anything at all to do with mysticism. In the Western world it has been a matter of debate what Buddhism should be called. It seems on the one hand to be an atheistic religion, on the other a kind of pragmatic ethics whose goal is freedom from suffering or even, if one considers how very important knowing has come to be for Buddhism, what could be called a philosophical religion. But none of these descriptions or any similar one really gets at its essence. One senses this at once on a closer study of the Pali canon. Nor could a description of this sort possibly get at its essence, if our thesis is right—that Buddhism aims in its inmost intention at "absolute transcendence." For absolute transcendence is precisely what cannot be brought under categories.

To drop the matter of a description's getting at the essence of a thing: if one asks what elements of mysticism older Buddhism contains, it is the idea of nirvana that seems more than anything else to point in that direction. For instance, Walter T. Stace writes in his *Teachings of the Mystics* . . .: ". . . Nirvana is the only mystical element in Buddhism, all other elements being rationalistic and skeptical."[4] Yet, if what we have said about the integrity of and necessary connection between the three basic thoughts is right, then the other two, the doctrine of *anatta* and the rejection of metaphysical judgements, must be mystical as well.

The doctrine of *anatta* has always been thought to be especially characteristic of Buddhism. Some attribute to it the special status of Buddhism among other contemporary and earlier philosophical and religious systems; others dispute this. In any case, the doctrine of *anatta*—and on this point everyone doubtless agrees—is what sets Buddhism apart, and so much so that, unless one has grasped the doctrine, one has no prospect of understanding Buddhism. In the canon Buddha himself calls it that part of his teachings which is difficult to grasp and which should be studied most, and so important a modern scholar of Buddhism as Edward Conze says: "One assumes that it will need more than one life-time to get to the bottom of it."[5] In general, it shows up the illusion that there is he whom I take myself to be when I refer back to myself.

Nowadays we have identity on the brain. To characterize the doctrine of *anatta* in a slogan: it is the gaining of identity by way of de-identification, and indeed of all and sundry. What does this mean? The salient elements in the concept of identity are unity and sameness, but they do not by any means constitute its essence. The word comes from the Latin *isdem* or *idem* and means just-he-ness or just-that-ness. An identity card proves its bearer to be just who he is. To have de-identified myself from everything means that there is no one and nothing, not even myself, about which I can say "I am he or that."

Older Buddhism reduced it to a formula, just as simple as it is unobjectionable, which recurs stereotypically in the canon. It is again and again shown that there is nothing of which one wouldn't have to say, if one conceives it properly, "This does not belong to me, this I am not, this is not my I."

---

[4] Mentor Book, 1960, p. 70.
[5] *Buddhism, its Essence and Development*, (Oxford: Bruno Cassirer, 1951), p. 19.

I shall set beside that a passage from a sermon which will at the same time exhibit Buddha's extraordinary ability to make his teaching clear with suggestive similes:

> "What do you think about this, monks? If a person were to gather or burn or do as he pleased with grass, twigs, branches and foliage in the Jeta Grove, would it occur to you: The person is gathering *us*, he is burning *us*, he is doing as he pleases with *us*?"
> "No, Lord. For it is not us nor what belongs to us."
> "Even so, monks, what is not yours, put it away; putting it away will be for a long time for your welfare and happiness. Corporeality, feeling, perception, the habitual tendencies and consciousness, monks, are not yours; put them away, putting them away will be for a long time for your welfare and happiness."[6]

One must mind the "If one conceives it properly . . ." It is indicative of the inner consistency of older Buddhism, which explicitly wishes to appeal to a very particular circle of persons only. If someone were to come along and say, "Though I can't regard a heap of twigs and branches and foliage as my I, I can my individuality," he wouldn't be viewing the matter correctly; that is to say, he wouldn't be endowed with right views. There would be, therefore, no sense in speaking with him further. In order to gain true views, he would first have to fulfill certain moral requirements, such as form a part of the Eightfold Path. If he were not even prepared to do that, one would have to send him on his way.

The proposition that the phenomenal world is without an I actually means, strictly speaking, that nothing in it is an I, because there is nothing in it worthy of being my I, or better, because there is nothing in it affording me a foothold or sufficiency that I can support myself on, not even me. Should I make something my I, as natural consciousness does of itself, I should fall into metaphysical illusion. Without complete inward presence of mind, without being mindful of myself, I shall inevitably identify myself with something. For this reason, mindfulness is the cardinal virtue among the Buddhists, and exercises in mindfulness take up a good deal of space in their doctrinal instruction.

To guard against a likely misunderstanding: to say that everything is without an I is not to say that there is no I. The two assertions become one only for a thinking which moves in the compass of everything and nothing and is not able to get beyond that.

If everything is without an I, there is no "being," no "substance," no "subject." Concepts like these are seen rather to be mere fictions of my thought and my imagination. A metaphysics that posits some ultimate on which to rest thus deprives itself of the least foundation.

---

[6] *The Collection of the Middle Length Sayings (Majjhima-Nikāya)*, vol. I, *The First Fifty Discourses (Mūlapannāsa)*, translated from the Pali by I. B. Horner (London: published for the Pali Text Society by Luzac & Company, Ltd., 1954), p. 181 ("Discourse on the Parable of the Water-Snake"). [The translation has been slightly altered to bring it in line with the German translation. (Tr.)]

With these last remarks we rise to a new level of reflection. It is well-known that Buddha declined to answer questions such as whether the world is eternal or not eternal, limited or not limited, whether the soul and body are the same or not the same, whether there is an existence after death or not, questions, in other words, which more or less make up the content of the *metaphysica specialis* of traditional school philosophy. Pupils and other monks had already reproached him for this—notably the monk Malunkyaputta and the wandering ascetic Vacchagotta—and Buddha answered the reproach in detail. The parable of the poisoned arrow has become the best known reply. Someone is hit by one, an able physician is sent for; the fellow who has been shot refuses, however, to let the arrow be removed until he knows who shot it, what sort of bow it was, what manner of arrowhead it is, and so on. Long before he had found all this out, he would have died of his wound or of poisoning. Just so, should someone want an answer to all the aforesaid questions before he followed Buddha's teachings on redemption from suffering.—That will be evident to everyone and also illustrates Buddha's extraordinary ability to create suggestive parables. Just the same, this parable has narrow limits, and one should especially note that Buddha always accommodates himself in his talks to his listeners' powers of comprehension.

Accordingly, it might appear that the reasons for his declining to engage in metaphysical discussion are, as we should say today, pragmatic. Others would say that they are positivistic in kind: metaphysical assertions like these are meaningless, or else that they are agnostic: to answer them goes beyond the powers of our human understanding. But these descriptions hardly get at the matter.

One must take note of Buddha's well-considered manner in declining to make metaphysical judgements. He does not say "I reject them." Rather, to the question, for instance, whether the world is limited, he replies: I do not say that the world is limited. All the logically possible answers are rehearsed with the same disavowal: I do not say that the world is not limited; I do not say that the world is neither limited nor not limited; I do not say that the world is limited as well as not limited.

The point is that, if I have not got any position at all on some matter I am disabled from stating even this fact; but there are things I can say to show that I have not got any position. Buddha does this in the way explained. It was left to scholars who did not understand this to admire, by a projection of their own behavior, the "skill" (Frauwallner) with which Buddha avoided metaphysical questions.

But why does Buddha not take a position on these questions? For one thing, he was not interested in them; not because he did not have any feeling for metaphysics, but because his interest was not in the world but in redemption from it. And then—and now we get to the heart of the matter—: there is no one here capable of making metaphysical judegments. Every judgement takes the form "I judge." Metaphysical judgements are illusory because, according to the *anatta* doctrine, the one making them is illusory. They have their origin in and particularly nourish the illusion of the I and self-conceit. We must apply to them too the principle, "This does not belong to me, this I am not, this is not my I." There are no total views I could support myself on in my innermost self.

When it is asked in the older texts, "Is the world limited?" "Is the world not limited?" "Is the world eternal?" "Is the world not eternal?" and both alternatives are rejected, the parallels with Kant and his cosmological antinomies force themselves by their very form on the Western reader. In the same way the *anatta* doctrine seems to have a certain relationship with Kant's distinction between appearance and the thing in itself, according to which I am to myself only appearance, and what I "myself" am is unknown to me and will always remain so. There are often references to this in writings on Buddhism. All the same, there are—apart from the difference of time and place—radical differences. In particular, the untouched ground of knowledge remains for Kant the "I think." To give it up and leave it behind lay outside his purview.

Older Buddhism lies entirely outside Heidegger's purview. His philosophy must be regarded as being wholly a product of Western thought-patterns (on account of the terrible general confusion[7] on this point a few words ought to be said about it), with a goodly measure of eccentricity. Eccentricity need not be a bad thing. Perhaps it is what is best in Heidegger's thought. To me at least, during forty years of more or less close association with Heidegger and on countless walks, his eccentricity seemed to be the magic of his personality. Heidegger's interest is in the world—and in nothing else. Transcendence in the sense here intended is foreign to him. His thinking has no more and no less to do with mysticism than have Japanese and Western Zen Buddhism; but for this fact it could not have come to a "dialogue" between them. Nowadays we would gladly be rid of the absolute. The entire Heideggerian philosophy is characterized by this desire, and it is only by keeping this in mind that we may legitimately criticize it. When, for instance, Heidegger closes his lecture "The Question Concerning Technology" with the obscure statement: "For putting questions is the piety of thought," he is saying something utterly unmystical.[8] Seen in terms of mysticism, it would have to be: Putting questions is the worldliness of thought. For mysticism the piety of thought would be to bring thought to the point where it casts off the putting of questions. This brings us back to Kant, whose thought is pious in this sense. For, once I know that essentially I can

---

[7] Cf., for example, John D. Caputo, *The Mystical Element in Heidegger's Thought* (Athens, Ohio: Ohio University Press, 1978). [Footnote added orally by the author after I lent him the book to read. (Tr.)]

[8] Heidegger himself had misgivings about this sentence. In *On the Way to Language*, translated by Peter D. Hertz (New York: Harper & Row, 1971), p.72, he says, "One of the exciting experiences of thinking is that at times it does not fully comprehend the new insights it has just gained and does not properly see them through. Such, too, is the case with the sentence just cited that questioning is the piety of thinking. The lecture ending with that sentence was already in the ambience of the realization that the true stance of thinking cannot be to put questions, but must be to listen to that which our questioning vouchsafes—and all questioning begins to be a questioning only in virtue of pursuing its quest for essential being." I leave it to the reader to decide whether his revised stance is in consonance with Struve or not. (Tr.)

know nothing, a limit has been put on questioning, and the road is clear for other things. And one could also say that Buddha's refusal to answer the metaphysical questions mentioned a bit ago must not be understood (as admittedly happened from time to time in older Buddhism) as if he in fact knew the answers but felt it inappropriate that his pupils know them. It is rather the case that he could not give answers without giving explanations as well, which, though not identical to those in the *Critique of Pure Reason*, would not have been a whit the less difficult and subtle. Not only did this seem to him a waste of time (as the parable of the arrow shows), but, above all, he could hardly have counted on his listeners' having the necessary talent. As already remarked, he always geared his talks precisely to their powers of comprehension.

This is especially the case with the third basic thought, to which I now turn: nirvana.—There will scarcely be any other Buddhist idea that is so familiar in the West, and just as everyone associates, for example, the underworld and crime with Chicago, so everyone associates nirvana immediately with Buddhism and wants to know what nirvana really is. Words and concepts, once debased, can never be rehabilitated. So it is in the West with the word "nirvana," which we continue, incorrigibly, to associate with the notion of nothingness. Nothingness need not be black; it can also be thought of as white. During a persistent snow storm in Arosa, Thomas Mann jots down on 3rd March 1934, "Snow nirvana." Schopenhauer confides at the close of the first volume of *The World as Will and Representation* with reference to the "Buddhaists" that what "remains after total annihilation of the will" is, "in fact, nothing," which we fear as children fear the dark, and from which we should "dispel" the "gloomy impression." And Max Beckmann's comment, written into the margin of his personal copy of Schopenhauer's book in Berlin on 15th October 1934, is "Yes, pleasant, a matter-of-fact mystic, a man." But do not such sayings lead us to the edge of a fatal heroism, which, while characteristic of the modern Western world, may safely be said to be at odds with ancient Indian civilization and with ancient civilizations in general?

"Nirvana" is not a philosophical or a metaphysical term in older Buddhism but rather a password of sorts—a password possessed of a peculiarly magical power—by which the like-minded travelers tracing a particular interior path recognize each other. Scholars, in their embarrassment, have recourse to the etymology of the word. "*Nirvanam,*" in Pali "*nibbanam,*" means to go out, as a fire or a flame goes out: an image often used in the canon. But for the ancient Indians, a fire did not at all cease to exist when it went out—as was long believed here in keeping with the Western mode of thought—; rather, it merely passed out of the phenomenal world and could no longer be grasped.[9] To "go out," then, in the case of the thought of "nirvana," is not to become absolutely nothing, which is as nonsensical an idea as it is trivial, but to disappear from the phenomenal world—in the case of *paranirvana,* for good.

---

[9] See E. Frauwallner, *Geschichte der indischen Philosophie*, vol. I, (Salzburg, 1953), pages 225ff.; D. Schlingloff, *Die Religion des Buddhismus*, vol. I, (Sammlung Göschen, vol. 174, Berlin, 1962), pp. 113f.

Though an interpretation like this one is certainly more adequate, it still only skirts one side of the issue, and the main problem has not even been caught sight of. For it might seem from what I have said that, from the moment of going out, a person "is" in some sort of a beyond or a nowhere in a way that we, at least, cannot fathom. "Einst werde ich liegen im Nirgend, bei einem Engel irgend" ("One day I shall lie in nowhere, with some angel," Paul Klee).[10] But notions like these land us back in some sort of metaphysics, from which we cannot extricate ourselves even with talk of "annulling the subject-object relation." Of Buddha, after he entered nirvana, the texts tell us rather that he has disappeared in such a way that one cannot even say that he no longer is. Let us dwell on the abyss of this thought for a moment in order to realize that nirvana cannot by any manner of means be "naturalized" into the realm of reflection and the language of objects, that the point is to leave this realm.

To make this clearer, something should be said (with the brevity circumstances demand) about meditation in older Buddhism. Older Buddhism distinguishes four levels of meditation, which always recur stereotypically in the canon.

1st level: Release from the sensible world. This leads to an inner joy and a sense of well-being. Reverie, in other words reflection, continues at this level.
2nd level: Reflection and deliberation are silenced. Out of this arises once again joy and a heightened inner well-being.
3rd level: This joy tapers off. A (transcendental) feeling of happiness streams in to take its place.
4th level: Release even from this feeling of happiness. Complete tranquility.

It is important to note that each level necessarily proceeds from the one before. The feeling of discontent, of deficiency, which is present through each of the first three levels, forces one to climb farther. And it is important to see that, although the difficulties grow progressively from level to level, and with them the temptation to take refuge in illusions, so, in the same measure, do one's abilities to overcome these difficulties grow.

These same four levels reappear, by the way, in Christian mysticism. Many may be better able to understand what I have been getting at by a consideration of these four levels here. Once again I list the four levels in slogan form, this time according to Johannes Evangelista of Hertogenbosch. He lived from 1588 to 1635. His main book, *Het Ryck Godts in der Zielen . . .*, (*The Kingdom of God in the Soul . . .*), was composed in Dutch and was printed for the first time in 1637, two years after his death. It appeared, as well as in English and Spanish translations, in various German editions, the first one in Sulzbach in 1665, the fifth and last one in Augsburg in 1848. So long as one doesn't let oneself be put

---

[10] Struve discusses this passage from Paul Klee in *Philosophie und Transzendenz* (1969), p. 119f., in the course of a discussion of *space*. (Tr.)

off by the dated language and title, one will discover to one's astonishment prescriptions for a meditation of unique subtlety.

Johannes Evangelista speaks of "four points":

1st point:	Taking leave of all created things, of all "creatures." But one has not yet taken leave of oneself.
2nd point:	Taking leave of myself. This leads to divine irradiation. Divine irradiation is not God, however, but a gift from God, and if I want this gift then I want it and not God.
3rd point:	Taking leave of God's gifts. Then I shall receive God himself as a gift and that means me.
4th point:	Taking leave even of God.

Yet let us return to older Buddhism. It is of decisive importance to see that the fourth and last level of meditation—emptiness and total tranquility—is not in itself nirvana or the state of nirvana, although it is from this fourth level and only from there that the transition to nirvana occurs,[11] and this transition is completely different from the transitions from one level of meditation to the next. It didn't take long before one no longer comprehended this and was content to reach the fourth or even a lower level of meditation. Nowadays there will be some, and they will not be few in number, who, if they half succeed in reaching the first level, will be sure they are already in a state of meta-nirvana, from which point of view they can regard nirvana critically. For one does begin to experience a certain feeling of happiness even before reaching the first level of meditation. But nirvana is not a psychological or a psychotherapeutic magnitude, though meditation at the first two levels can be in some degree. The fourth level is not like state of trance, but rather a state of utmost inner wakefulness and presence of mind, as is required to bring about the ultimate and authentic transition.

---

[11] Regarding the two branches of meditation, see what Struve has to say in *On the Nonconformity of the Real*, below, p. 54: *Samadhi* meditation "leads to a state of complete inward peace and release . . . As a liberation from the world it is related to the world, is 'mundane', not 'transcendental' . . . It is otherwise with clear sight (*vipassana*), which is the other great area of [Buddhist] meditation and which is the prerequisite for entry into nirvana and thus transcendental in kind." See also Karl Seidenstücker, *Pāli Buddhismus in Übersetzungen*, 2nd ed. (München-Neubiberg: Oskar Schloss, 1923), p. 275, ". . . For entry into *nibbāna*, *vipassanā* is always necessary, while *samatha* with its requisites (the levels of meditation) cannot bring about entry into the higher path, let alone into *nibbāna*"; and Nyanaponika, *Geistestraining durch Achtsamkeit: Die buddhistische Satipaṭṭhāna-Methode*, 3rd ed. (Konstanz: Christiani, 1984), p. 73ff., where he speaks of reaching *vipassana* by first going through the levels of *jhāna* in *samadhi* meditation and of "pure clear sight," which presupposes merely the "bordering level of composure" before attaining clear sight. In both cases *vipassana* is necessary for entry into nirvana. A version of Nyanaponika's book exists in English: *The Heart of Buddhist Meditation* (Rider & Co.: London, 1962). (Tr.)

Nirvana is not a psychological magnitude, but neither is it a cosmological magnitude. Especially instructive in this matter is a famous "Udana" of Buddha's, a sentence-like ceremonial declaration in which a term of knowledge is revealed in an "instantaneous illumination." It reads:

> There is, monks, a not-born, a not-become, a not-made, a not-caused. If, monks, that unborn, not become, not-made, uncaused were not, there would be apparent no escape for this here that is born, become, made, caused. But since, monks, there is an unborn, a not-become, a not-made, an uncaused, therefore the escape for this here that is born, become, made, caused is apparent.[12]

In its whole manner, even in its diction, this seems reminiscent of early Greek thought. Buddha lived about 500 B. C., that is, was more or less a contemporary of Parmenides and Heraclitus, in whom early Greek though culminates. Anaximander, the first early Greek thinker from whom a written word has come down to us, inaugurates Western philosophy, as it were, with the utterance: ἀρχὴ τῶν ὄντων τὸ ἄπειρον, origin of things that are is the unbounded. Since Anaximander, the following line of reasoning has been repeated in countless variants: Everything that is, is bounded. What is bounded requires a ground. The ground must be different from the things it grounds. Therefore, everything that is must have a ground that is not itself bounded and that cannot be similar in kind to what is bounded.

Now what seems uncommonly instructive about Buddha's saying is that it *does not* proceed to a conclusion in the same way, and that it does not say: "Because there is something that has bounds, there must be an unbounded as its ground." He says rather that there must be an unbounded, because otherwise there would be no redemption for what has bounds.—That is something entirely different. The unborn, not-become, etc. is not brought into a causal relation to the born, become, etc. If it were, Buddha would be setting up a transcendent absolute and would be slipping into a mode of the very metaphysical thought he is trying to guard against; but this is insured against by the use of the fourfold "not." What Buddha says is neither ontological nor cosmological but rather "soteriological." "Redemption" is the central and only theme of Buddhism. Redemption—from what? From being perishable.—

Nirvana is no *arche*; it is not conceived of as the origin of man and his world. It has nothing at all to do with that, though man has something to do with it, since he strives to go over to it and into it. It cannot, therefore, be grasped by way of negation, but eludes all attempts at defining it, as it must, if what was said before about meditation holds true. Thought of objects is overcome and left behind at the second level of meditation.—Of course, that accomplishment is by no means adequate to solve modern Western man's problems; everything in him

---

[12] *The Minor Anthologies of the Pali Canon. Part II. Udāna: Verses of Uplift AND Itivuttaka: As It Was Said,* translated by F. L. Woodward, with an introduction by Mrs Rhys Davids (London: Geoffrey Cumberlege, Oxford University Press, 1948), p. 98 (*Ud.* VIII 3).

resists the solution. More of this in a moment.

First let us pause to catch our breath and say a word about the images of Buddha. If absolute transcendence defies every attempt at categorizing it, whether directly or indirectly, then it will also defy any attempt to present it. And early Buddhist art may well be of no mean importance for a mental comprehension of absolute transcendence. Deep down inside, Westerners no doubt find the ubiquitous Buddha statues comical. Many may have thought to themselves what Schopenhauer's rigidly Catholic housekeeper, Margarethe Schnepp, exclaimed when Schopenhauer was sent a gilt Buddha from Paris in 1856: "Why, he sits there like a tailor!" "And he isn't even tailoring," one might add. "He has his hands in his lap and does nothing. Ridiculous."

As to doing nothing: older Buddhism does not assign any moral value to work. Monks were forbidden to work. This, by the way, is an essential difference between Eastern and Western monasticism. It does not, however, mean that Buddhism came out in favor of indolence. Just the opposite. Look up the "Greater Discourse at Assapura" in the *Collection of the Middle Length Sayings* with the constant refrain: "for there is something further to be done!" This sutta is, by the way, a compendium of Buddhist teaching.[13] Schopenhauer flew into a rage and upbraided his housekeeper: "You gross person, that's how you speak of the victoriously exalted one! Have I ever blasphemed your Lord God?" But this shows that he had not yet progressed much beyond a "Buddhism for Europeans," as his "pupil" Nietzsche puts it.

In truth, the images of Buddha, particularly the older ones, are not, as one might expect at first, naturalistic likenesses of persons meditating. Photographs of statues of Buddha with Indian Yogis of the same type sitting next to them, such as we sometimes run across, make that quite clear. They are not idealized examples for meditators either. Perhaps, in a certain way, the depictions of the *arhants*, the disciples of Buddha, are idealized examples. It is precisely when we compare these statues to those of Buddha that we see how completely different the latter are. They are realistic symbols, and as such are admittedly intended to promote and encourage meditation. They are always stylized into the type of a meditator. Because the material structure is in this case an abstraction and a fiction, it is able to serve as a symbol of transcendence. The human form has symbolic force because only man is capable of absolute transcendence.

Statues of the Gypta Period in Indian art and of the Wei Period in early Chinese art have this character to a high degree, and one can by a consideration of these statues very clearly trace the historically necessary process in which they become shallow and superficial: from absolute to relative transcendence, from relative transcendence to immanence and then on to empty imitation which leads to serial production in workshops and finally to mechanical production in factories, so that each piece is "identical" to every other. The image of Buddha has today its own kind of contemplative existence in warehouses and knick-knack shops.

---

[13] In *Middle Length Sayings*, (cited in note 6), vol. 1, pp. 325-334.

We shall now turn to Western mysticism. It is characteristic of my lecture that I have nothing of substance to say that would go beyond the first part, and yet it is just now that the lecture will become really interesting, sometimes as gripping as a detective story. It is incumbent on us to recognize and overcome what is conventional in the talk about absolute transcendence, so far as it is at all possible.

The great line of division seems at first sight to be that Western mysticism, as a whole, thinks theologically. Older Buddhism is, as is well-known, atheistic: not in the sense that it denies the existence of the gods of traditional religion, but in the sense that it does not acknowledge any god as the ultimate principle and source of all things. In my opinion, however, the real difference is not to be sought here but must be sought in the fact that Western mysticism thinks philosophically. That Western mysticism thinks theologically is merely a consequence of its thinking philosophically. This is especially noticeable when we consider that both its most prominent representatives, Plotinus and Meister Eckhart, are marked by an uncontrollable urge to understand and know speculatively. Eckhart's influence on the formation of German philosophical terminology is well-known.—Plotinus is perhaps the only major mystic who did not belong to a religious community and did not found one, yet he did not, for all that, think independently, but considered himself a pupil of Plato's and a reviver of his philosophy. Plato, however, is regarded as the author and founder of what we call philosophy in the pregnant sense of the word.

The question forces itself upon us: Is mysticism an element of Plato's thought and, if it is, how important an element? I think a very definite answer can be given—and it is clear that it will be of decisive importance in the sequel. It is: There is not a trace of absolute transcendence in Plato's thought, though doubtless there is an element of relative transcendence.

If we take our bearings from Plato's written work—and we may do nothing else here—it is of all the dialogues the *Symposium*, more precisely the last part of Diatima's speech, that tends most markedly towards mysticism. The three-stage ascent described there, at the end of which the cross over and leap to the "beautiful itself" occurs, has become, at any rate for subsequent Western mysticism, an example quoted again and again.

Yet it is plainly a matter of relative transcendence, as strongly as a mystical undertone can also be felt there. Beautiful things are bound to the Beautiful by participation. This becomes completely clear in the *Republic*, where the Good—identical with the Beautiful—is explicitly described as and shown to be the origin of the universe (511b). —Plato's Socrates does say in a famous passage, which has been like a beacon for mystics ever since, that the Good is not being, but surpasses even being in dignity and power (509b). The Good, as the foundation of the ideas and of beings, cannot *be* in the same sense as these latter are; yet there is no question that Plato conceives of the Good as having form, and so not as unconditionally transcendent. As much as Plato may have emphasized in certain passages in his dialogues that the Good is beyond being, that the Good is *not* the origin and ground of everything lies outside his purview.

But it lies outside Plotinus's purview as well. It is true he pushes the beyondness of the *Agathon* to its limit by reasoning, with an unheard of and new earnestness, from the philosophical premise that the source and what springs from the source must differ. However, the possibility that the "primeval One," which for Plotinus is strictly amorphous[14] and ineffable, might *not* be the source of all things, is never considered for a moment. Rather, the entire cosmos emanates out of the primeval One through the well-known series of hypostases.

It is probably Dionysius Areopagita, whose thought is directly dependent on Proclus, who went the farthest in this direction. His *Negative Theology*, composed about 500 A. D., became the main source of Christian mysticism during the Middle Ages and thereafter. In a grandiose manner—for instance in the 5th chapter of his *Theologia Mystica*—he negates all positive and negative predications of God—except one, whose validity he acknowledges in the extremist manner and unconditionally: that God is "the perfect and sole cause of all things." The *via causativa*, far from being impaired by the *via negativa*, is actually reinforced.

Yet there is a noteworthy exception. That is the Christian Gnostic Marcion, who lived in the second century. Adolf von Harnack has devoted an important scholarly monograph to him: *Marcion. Das Evangelium vom fremden Gott: Eine Monographie zur Grundlegung der katholischen Kirche* (Leipzig, 1921). In the preface Harnack says that Marcion is "the only thinker in Christendom who never wavered in the conviction that the Deity that redeems man from the world has simply nothing to do with the Deity of cosmology and cosmic theology." Harnack is mistaken. There is, in my opinion, one other who is as unwavering as Marcion in this conviction, and that is Meister Eckhart. At all events, he is so in a few extreme passages in his German sermons.

Marcion's teachings were rejected by the Roman Synod in 144 as "a heresy of the worst kind," and he himself was excommunicated. Dionysius Areopagita's teachings were declared orthodox at the Lateran Council of 649. The Church prosecuted Meister Eckhart in 1326.

Yet Marcion is a Gnostic, not a mystic. It is true that the unknown "other God" he speaks of is "foreign" to this world and its creator, but this God is himself conceived of as the creator of invisible realities.[15] Eckhart takes this otherness seriously in an incomparably more profound way, and it is here that the immense intellectual difference between the two can be seen. Even Eckhart, as a philosophically thinking man of the Christian Middle Ages, everywhere is guided primarily by the notion of God as the creator of the world. However, there is besides this notion a further distinction that gains staggering significance for him: the one between Godhead and God. The Godhead is God as he is in himself, and as distinct from the God of the Trinity, from God as he is for what he has created. The Godhead is "hidden," is utterly incomprehensible to the understanding. Only identity (in the sense adumbrated earlier) can be predicated of God as Godhead: he is who he is, whereas the God of creation can be known by

---

[14] See *Enneads*, VI. 7. 32. 9: αρχη δε το ανείδεον. (Tr.)
[15] Harnack, *Marcion: Das Evangelium vom fremden Gott*, p. 91.

the creation in the Trinitarian process.

The distinction between Godhead and God is a product of the Scholastic tradition and did not originate with Eckhart. What is without precedent, in my opinion, is the way in which Eckhart radicalizes this fundamental distinction in certain passages of his German sermons. And this he invariably does with a passion that strikes one as almost extravagant. And so it is at the end of the "Little Castle" sermon, whose text is one of those best assured through plenty of copies, and which is one most characteristic of Eckhart, and also in the sermon "*Noli timere eos*," which closes with the words, "If anyone has understood this sermon, I wish him well! If no one had come to listen, I should have had to preach it to the offering box. There are, however, certain poor people who will return home and say: 'Henceforth I shall stay in my own place and eat my own bread and serve God in peace.' I say, by the eternal truth, that these people will have to remain in their errors, for they will never attain what those attain who follow after God in poverty and exile! Amen."[16]

Earlier in this sermon Eckhart had said "I beseech you to understand this in terms of eternal truth, the everlasting truth, and by my soul. So I shall say something further that I have never said before. God and the Godhead are as different from each other as heaven and earth."[17] And a bit further on: "Thus creatures speak of God—but why do they not mention the Godhead? Because there is only unity in the Godhead and there is nothing to talk about. God acts. The Godhead does not. It has nothing to do and there is nothing going on in it. It never is on the lookout for something to do."[18] Here and in a number of other passages the difference between Godhead and God is brought to such a high pitch that it is almost only the analogous designation that holds the two together, and "the Godhead which redeems has nothing more to do with the God who creates the world." The intensity of his unique experience, an unmistakable inner knowledge—and it is in this sense that the emphatic assurances such as "by the eternal truth," "by my soul," which occur without fail in such passages in the sermons, are to be understood—constrain Eckhart to explode and abandon the traditional and conventional formulae and ways of understanding and to say things that just had to give offense and bring him into fatal conflict with a society and church that wants to extend its worldly power.

I would like to shed light on these matters from yet another angle. Plato, in the peculiarly extravagant "digression" in the middle of the *Theaetetus*, the dialogue with which he opens the second phase of his philosophical activity, put what was closest to his heart and the goal towards which his thought aimed into a simple formula: ὁμοίωσις θεῷ κατὰ τὸ δυνατόν, "becoming like God so far as possible" (176b).

---

[16] *Meister Eckhart: A Modern Translation*. By Raymond Bernard Blakney (New York: Harper & Row, 1941), p. 226. (Tr.)

[17] Ibid., page 225, but reading *iemar wernder* in accordance with the text Struve has and translating accordingly 'everlasting' instead of Blakney's 'ever-receding': Blakney had only Pfeiffer's 19th century edition of Eckhart at his disposal. (Tr.)

[18] Ibid., p. 226. (Tr.)

Is this formula mystical? No. The corresponding mystical formulation would read: ἕνωσις θεῷ, "becoming one with God."—What is the difference? Plato's formula asks that man should, so far as it is possible, assimilate what is to what is considered good and perfect. Or, to simplify a bit, that a man should improve himself and the world so far as he is able. The formula is idealistic, nay, states the essence of idealism in an extremely simple way. One sees here, incidentally, that all so-called materialism is thoroughly idealistic.

The mystical formula is different. The qualification "so far as one is able" is missing. For I can become one with something only completely or not at all. Further, what is meant by "becoming one" is not some sort of material or personal unification or merging. The point is not that I should try to make myself perfect and, so far as it is possible, to transform myself into God; rather it is that I should take leave of myself and seize what I am not, the real, just as it reveals itself.

Mysticism is not and never has been idealistic; it is realistic. When, for instance, Eckhart writes in his *Book of Divine Comfort*, "Therefore, when betimes it is the will of God that I commit sin, I shall not afterward wish that I had not done it, for thus God's will is done on earth . . .,"[19] he is being profoundly realistic. This passage belongs to those incriminated in the papal bull "In agro dominico" of 27th March 1329.

We no longer take offence at this passage—not as much. We do not want perfection, we want reality. Idealism, in the sense presented, has today become a highly questionable affair. The great critic of idealism in our time is Nietzsche; and who could overlook how wonderfully akin he and Eckhart are, in spite of all the differences that can be ascribed to the interval between their lives: the creativity and the mastery both had in handling the German language, the enormous inner intensity with which they put their whole selves into what they think, the extremeness and consistency of their thought, the boldness, the paradoxical, the contradictory, the extravagance, the provocativeness, the brilliance, the manifold iridescence of expression, and finally the way life and the mystery of life become for them the great moving theme.—Nietzsche saw very clearly that traditional idealism is illusory in terms of knowledge and utopian in terms of being, and he also showed how, by making basic misjudgments about the essence of reality, it leads to the defamation of sensuality, irreverence for nature, and with that to what Nietzsche thought out in its historical meaning as nihilism. In popular terms, improvement of the world is in its very essence only seemingly an improvement, and leads not to heaven but to hell. It is for having seen all this that Nietzsche is the unique critic of the Western world that he is.

I shall make clearer what I have said by way of an elucidation of mysticism's fundamental concept, taking leave. Having taken leave or detachment is the basic theme of Meister Eckhart's sermons and of those of subsequent German mysticism from Suso, Tauler, Ruysbroeck to the "*Theologica Germanica.*"

He has taken leave, according to mysticism, who has taken leave of himself and the world and has committed himself to God. Leave first in the sense of

---

[19] Ibid., p. 50. (Tr.)

letting something go, and then leave in the sense of leaving oneself or committing oneself to something. The antonym of leave is accept.

Having taken leave and the concomitant peace should not be confused with indifference. If I am indifferent to a thing I am of a certainty establishing a relation to it by my very indifference. For instance, one speaks of punishing someone with indifference. But having taken leave is the relinquishing of relations. This cannot be thought. Having taken leave is therefore paradoxical and must be so. Otherwise it would be just one worldly disposition among others. The world does not in any way vanish for him who has taken leave: on the contrary, it gains for him a new reality of unheard of matter-of-factness: he does not accept it, he does not reject it, he is not indifferent to it.—One could distinguish between being interested, uninterested and disinterested. Having taken leave would then be disinterestedness, indifference in the high sense, but not indolence. (In the English-speaking world someone coined the expression non-attachment, in distinction from attachment and unattachment.)

Disinterest in oneself and the world is, however, only one side of taking leave: the other is turning towards what is not the world, in committing oneself to God: and the latter is the reason for the former.

Taking leave of oneself and the world and committing oneself to God: one can see that this formula with its triad soul, world, God derives from Christian mediaeval thought, and is cosmologically and theologically oriented.—But here the extraordinary thing about Meister Eckhart once again becomes apparent: that he does not stop there but goes on to burst this conventional arrangement of things and gets beyond them. For in the sermon "*Qui audit me*," the so-called "sermon on taking leave," at the conclusion of which he coins the German adjective "*gelassen*" right in the course of the presentment, he says, "Man's last and highest parting occurs when, for God's sake, he takes leave of God."[20]

This sentence is just as paradoxical as it is provocative. One should not attempt to take that away from it. Long ago "for God's sake" eroded into an empty phrase: "for God's sake, don't do that!" Eckhart's sentence aims at what was explained earlier: one should, for the Godhead's sake, that is, for the sake of God as he is in himself, take leave of God the Trinitarian creator, God as he is for the creation. If I do that I shall, by abandoning all theological and cosmological ideas, be preparing myself for the step and passage to a region having nothing more do with God and world in the customary sense.

So, what is meant is that one should take leave of God for the Godhead's sake. But Eckhart did not put it just that way. He also did not put God in the first position in quotation marks; indeed, he did not write this but spoke it. And so it must remain: taking leave of God for God's sake. Only in this way does the paradox retain its scathing pungency. Otherwise we would bring everything back into the region of objective ideas—which is only too familiar to us—where we take everything and nothing seriously. With this paradox Eckhart achieves an "atheism" which is so little conventional as that of older Buddhism and as that of Plotinus and as that of Nietzsche, and we arrive where we truly want to get:

---

[20] Ibid., p. 204. (Tr.)

beyond East and West, to the "foothills of Eternity," as an old mystic script has it.[21]

My lecture could end with that. But have we not strayed altogether too far from the here and now? We had better return to the present. And what could be better than a newspaper to pull us back to the present, and what paper better for us here than the *"B. Z."*?[22] And what could be more reassuring than a weekend supplement? Yet the article I should like to talk about in conclusion is not reassuring at all. Its title is "Will It All Be Over In 5,000 Years?"

That is some question. Here is how it is: As most everyone knows, our solar system is not stationary, but is moving through space at a speed of over 62,500 miles an hour. (The speed limit in the universe, our motor-car drivers will be comforted to hear, is 186,000 miles a second.) Now it could come to pass that our solar system will in the course of its travels one day collide with other stars, or find itself in a nebula, or something else. This too has been known for some time. But till recently the likelihood of such a catastrophe has been reckoned to be slight. However—and this is where the newspaper story comes in—after observing outer space and the distribution and density of the interstellar mass for the past eight years via the American research satellite "Copernicus," scientists have come to some alarming conclusions. Our solar system is moving away from a region with an extremely rarefied interstellar mass and towards a "dark cloud" whose interstellar mass is fifty thousand times denser. Our solar system will reach this dark cloud in roughly 5,000 years. For a start, less sunlight will reach the earth when this happens, and a new ice age will set in. There is a chance, however, that, with the help of a highly advanced technology, mankind will manage to survive a new ice age by "going underground." "But as soon as the center of the dark cloud is reached, the end of mankind will be inevitable." For the solar wind would suffocate, with the result that the sun would draw to itself the remaining atmosphere, at which time it would experience an immense increase in luminary strength and burn up everything on earth.

That some time or other all life on earth will be destroyed has, as I have said, long been known. What is new is the plethora of details the data provide and the exact point in time, to know which is made possible by satellite research; and the short time before this catastrophe is to take place is a surprise. For, in astronomical measure, five thousand years is an infinitesimally short time, and even in the earth's measure, whose age is today estimated to be about five billion years. The title of the article really ought to be: "Will Everything Be Over in a *Mere* Five Thousand Years?"—

But I did not cite this article on account of the astronomical data. Indeed, it talks about many other things as well. What is this supposed to mean, that everything is going to be over? A hit song that was sung in the Thirties comes to mind: "In fifty years everything will have gone by, in fifty years everything will

---

[21] '*in dem vorhove ewiger selikeit*' (Seuse [Suso], ed. by Bihlmeyer, p. 234); '. . . *ein vorstat des ewigen oder der ewikeit*' (*Theol. Germ.*, ed. by Mandel, p. 91).

[22] The *Badische Zeitung*, the main newspaper of Freiburg and the surrounding area. (Tr.)

be over . . ." ("In fünfzig Jahren ist alles vorüber, in fünfzig Jahren ist alles vorbei . . ."*).* No doubt there was a political reference to the "millennium" of the National Socialists in the song. — Everything is not over yet, as far as I am concerned. Fifty years, a thousand years, five thousand years—what does it matter!

But what is it supposed to mean, that everything is going to be over? Surely, everyone, whether he has cultivated his mind or not, whether he thinks philosophically or not, knows exactly what is meant—in fact, the author states it very appropriately and very bluntly. But is what is meant itself clear? And so we find ourselves landed back with our problem—transcendence and absolute transcendence.

When I say "everything will be over," whither do I transcend? Try to picture this sometime, but watch out that you do not get dizzy and have everything spinning in your head.

The astronomical perspectives are already "too high" for the everyday newspaper reader. A woman in Freiburg who lets rooms to students drew her face into thoughtful wrinkles, blinked and had this to say about the article: "I hardly think I'll still be alive in five thousand years." Evidently even the author of the article believed he ought to get back to the here and now. For he ends his article with the words: "The only hope is that, after crossing through the dark cloud, life on earth could begin again at the zero-point, and then maybe a race of men will emerge endowed with somewhat more intelligence and sense than its predecessor." How reasonable and clever, and yet, what a sad and dreary piece of wisdom! What perspectives and standards! The author, Victor Kunzemüller, passes judgment on the entire human race in the *"B.Z."* of 9th February 1980. And can a thinking man, if he turns over such things in his mind, avoid the question, And what then? Why this new race of men endowed with "somewhat more intelligence and sense," which will also not live on "forever"?

But if he does not avoid these questions, they can serve as an impetus to a different relation to the world. He will not deceive himself in a miserable, banal and arrogant manner by viewing contemporary humanity as not intelligent and decent enough, but will achieve an inner stance where he will know himself to be sheltered and where every cosmic catastrophe will lose all meaning for him: not because he will no longer be living when it comes, but because it will be for him in truth nothing real.

Even the most plausible and sober scholarly discussion lives from certain metaphors and general ideas and addresses us only by their means. The expression "dark cloud" may well be borrowed from mysticism: from Dionysius the Areopagite, *The Cloud of Unknowing* and John of the Cross. The conceptions of the end of the world such as have occupied humanity in sagas, myths, speculations on nature and science since the beginning of time have proved to be "oddly similar" (M. B. Weinstein). Not that that proves their truth or untruth: but it does show that they spring from a similar faculty of production and a similar behavior of natural man.—The theory and research in evolution teaches us that man has raised himself above the animals by developing and using tools and with them achieved dominion over nature and the other creatures. Seen in this way, *homo technicus* would be just as consistent a development of *homo rationalis* as this is of *homo bestialis*.

But since time immemorial *homo mysticus* has stood by the side of *homo technicus*.—Admittedly, ideas and reflections like these do not seriously enter into consideration for him: they are nothing real for him, because he is nothing real to himself. And his peace of mind does not rest on his being indifferent, because he has recognized that what is inalienable—that which cannot be spared—and what is inevitable—that which cannot be avoided—are the same.

Once again an identity I would like to close with.

On the Nonconformity of the Real

To speak of the nonconformity of the real seems like a dubious undertaking. Yet it must be done. On the one hand, we necessarily end up sounding banal, if we want to be intelligible; on the other hand, we inevitably fall into indissoluble contradictions and antinomies, which give everyone license to refute what has been said. And it would indeed be useless unless the experience, which is ostensibly under discussion here, is itself exhibited through such an undertaking, and unless through occupying oneself with the contradictions and antinomies into which this experience places one the senses are wakened and sharpened for it. But it is not only the wakening and sharpening of certain senses which we have all been endowed with but which mostly lie dormant and undeveloped in us that is at stake: ultimately at stake are certain inner enactments. It is only with these that effort in speech and thought attain their goal.

Very generally, we can say: we can speak and think naïvely or in a reflected manner or dialectically. A classical example from theology: "God is great" would be spoken naïvely. "God is the greatest being" would be spoken in a reflected manner. "God is great and is also not great" would be spoken dialectically. We are not accustomed to dialectical trains of thought—which we have no use for in everyday life—and they have something peculiarly irritating about them, something that undermines our accustomed ways of thinking: they're mostly cause for vexation.

The naïve appears dilettantish viewed from the point of view of the reflected; the reflected appears empty and boring viewed from the point of view of the dialectical. This not least of all because the absolute plays a role in everything dialectical, while the absolute remains excluded with the reflected mode of thought, and it is precisely this that its security rests on. The reflected is the "reasonable" *par excellence* in the general sense in which we use the word nowadays. As such, it can always count on implicit and still more on express appreciation and approval.

We can only speak of the nonconformity of the real naïvely or dialectically and must, to do that, continuously jump from the one to the other. The naïve should no more be underestimated than it should be overestimated. The sentence: "The real is the nonconforming" is naïve. Yet we must take it as the basis of our considerations and keep it in mind during the entire lecture like a ferry or raft which we let carry us and bring us farther. This image is, by the way, old. It is of no less significance for Plato than it is in Indian thought.[1] Once we have reached the goal, we shall not only leave this raft, but we shall burn it.[2] This assertion will constantly be challenged through dialectics. Conformity is a concept of relation, and the question arises: what doesn't reality conform to? The answer would be: to itself and to other things. Already here the simple assertion annuls itself.

If we can only speak of the nonconformity of the real in a naïve or dialectical fashion, that doesn't in any way mean that we can do without the reflective mode. The reflective is the element of philosophical thought, at least of contemporary philosophical thought, and indeed in order to join in with this discussion and thus be intelligible, we need it.

Therefore, I shall begin with some reflections on the concept of nonconformity. After these introductory remarks, I shall in the first part of my lecture cite and discuss a few historical examples of and testimonials to the experience of the nonconformity of the real from Eastern and Western thought. This experience is indeed as old and as widespread as human knowledge of reality is generally, and is inseparable from this. The course of its history indeed never goes in a straight line, but moves in twists and turns, which are not events that can be rationally illuminated. A process of ever-increasing consciousness and reflection takes place alongside it. This means that the experience in question here is most powerful and immediate in the oldest testimonials: we can no longer reproduce this experience in the same way today. But, in place of that, the experience has in the more recent and most recent testimonials gained in sharpness. Indeed, hasn't humanity closed ranks in a sort of camaraderie in order to continue existing in the face of this experience?

In the second half of my lecture, I shall build on these historical recollec-

---

[1] See Plato, *Phaedo* 85c-d: σχεδία. Struve, commenting on this in "Eine geschichtliche Erinnerung zum Thema: 'Erfahrung und Metaphysik,'" *Proceedings of the XIth International Congress of Philosophy*, Vol. IV, *Experience and Metaphysics* (1953), p. 132, says, "But even this raft is not found lying about but must itself be continuously brought forth by the one whom it will carry. Whoever seeks a firm, demonstrable and permanent base, such as logistics and the positivistic sciences attempt, fails to recognize the proper essence of philosophical experience. Philosophy is always without a base, but is not for that reason groundless. Usually we know ground only as base." (Tr.)

[2] See Wolfgang Struve, *Spuren und Stürze: Aufzeichnungen aus Skizzenbüchern 1984-1987*, #220: "Everything is an expedient. One must be ruthless with expedients. Once one has crossed over, one should not take the raft with one, rather, one must burn it." Wittgenstein also famously said in the *Tratatus Logico-Philosophicus:* "He must so to speak throw away the ladder, after he has climbed up on it" (6.54). Translated by F. P. Ramsey and C. K. Ogden with help from Wittgenstein (London: Routledge & Kegan Paul, 1922). (Tr.)

tions by adding some further considerations, though not in the sense of a systematic discussion: there are no insights of the sort that I could support myself on. The attempt should simply be made to get away from familiar modes of thought and reflection, and from various angles gain access, as much as possible, to those foreign and disconcerting primordial facts. In any case, we can only concern ourselves with what's important obliquely. If we were to make it our main object, it would elude us.

First of all, a brief exposition of the concept of nonconformity would be in order. To start with the most important point: this concept expresses a non-correspondence, which cannot merely be traced back to difference or otherness, but is abysmal and fathomless, and in its own way it possesses a scathing sharpness and a power defying thought. Our task now is to clarify this step by step.

Conforming, literally "forming along with," contains as its main component the philosophical primordial and fundamental word "form." The German "*Form*," borrowed from the Latin, was at first "used only of the human form,"[3] but then soon was extended to everything. What appears does so in a form, whereby this may be more or less distinct. "I am not in form today," a jogger says as he passes by me panting while I am taking a stroll through the forest. "Matter and form" are opposed and correlated concepts of fundamental importance in the philosophy of Aristotle and of the Middle Ages. You will recollect how Kant, for instance, speaks of space and time as "forms" of intuition. Yet form is not merely a term in the schools of philosophy. How far it reaches into our collective life-world can be seen in phrases und expressions such as reform, uniform, formal, a form that one fills out, formality, formalism, form (as a verb), formulate.

Thus conformism is a well-known catchword in our time too. In *Knaurs Lexicon* I find the "formulation": it is "the striving towards adaptation to prevailing customs, views and social and political conditions." (Edition of 1985. It's not found in the 1932 edition.)

Adaptation (*adaption*) is, as is well known, a concept which has gained considerable importance in biology since Lamarck and was introduced into sociology by Spencer. It refers to the alteration of a living being through the influence of the environment and to the adaptation to this environment, whereby generally the superiority of humans to other living beings is referred back to their "being the most adaptable living beings,"[4] and "the progress of mankind consists according to this in its ever more complete adaptation to social conditions."[5] Indeed, much could be said about it, and much could be brought up to counter it. Already Nietzsche sharply criticized the "shopkeeper's philosophy of

---

[3] Trübner's *Deutsches Wörterbuch*.
[4] *Philosophisches Wörterbuch*. Begründet von Heinrich Schmidt. 11th edition, völlig neu bearbeitet von Julius Streller, Stuttgart 1951.
[5] *Wörterbuch der philosophischen Begriffe*. Edited by Johannes Hoffmeister. 2nd edititon. Hamburg 1955.

Mr. Spencer,"[6] who was his contemporary: with his definition of life as a more and more efficient adaptation to external conditions he ignores its essence, its *will to power,* and overlooks the essential priority of "the spontaneous, aggressive, expansive, form-giving forces that give new interpretations and directions, although 'adaptation' follows only after this."[7] Put in modern terms: Humans don't merely alter themselves by adapting to the environment, but they also alter their environment, adapt it to themselves and to their needs. This last phenomenon has been occurring today in such an encompassing manner that we are becoming rather uneasy about it. These burning contemporary issues demonstrate that adaptation contains positive as much as negative elements. As for these elements within society, one could actually say that society's existence and health depend on the right relation between conformity and inconformity.

These things being as delicate and precarious as they are, we would do well briefly to discuss a particularly difficult and complex example, which will at the same time lead us to our proper theme, that is, the relation of the visual arts to the public and to society.[8]

An artist, if he be a true one, follows, when he brings forth his works, an inescapable, very definite inner compulsion, whereby we leave the question open what power this compulsion comes from and which laws, historical or other, this power is itself subject to. As personal as the productions of a major artist may be, this power is yet an impersonal one, and it is through just this impersonality that his creations attain a general validity and possess a certain normative character. However, it could be that through these productions he comes into an oppositional relationship to the society in which he produces and on whose material support, but also on whose ideal recognition he depends. This can even lead to a life and death conflict, as was the case during the National Socialist regime in Germany. And we may not comfort ourselves by saying that these times are past. Rather, the generality, the "broad public," is still unfavorably disposed to what one calls "modern art." Its measure of a work of art is its objectivity and "naturalness."

Expressionism, which for a long time [in Germany] was considered synonymous with modern art, might serve as more than just an example. At first, it was sharply rejected not only by the public, but even by the art critics, then gradually found recognition among them after the First World War and, with that, entrance into the museums, until the National Socialist upheaval put a sudden and violent end to all that. The works were not only branded as "degenerate art" and removed from public collections, the artists, inasmuch as they had held teaching posts, dismissed, but in many instances a ban on painting was imposed;

---

[6] *The Will to Power* 382. Translated by Walter Kaufmann and R. J. Hollingdale. Edited by Walter Kaufmann (New York: Random House, Inc., 1967 Vintage Books, 1968), p. 206. (Tr.)

[7] *On the Genealogy of Morals* II 12. Translated by Walter Kaufmann and R. J. Hollingdale (New York: Random House, 1967), p.79.

[8] On the following, *see* especially Wilhem Worringer, *Problematik der Gegenwartskunst*, München 1948.

indeed, Hitler threatened them in a major speech with castration. A society that proceeds in this way with what does not conform to it passes judgement on itself.

Today the importance of expressionism is no longer in dispute; publications on it and exhibitions abound, especially as of late. But does it find general recognition? I hardly think so. It may well be, for instance, that an industrialist collects expressionistic graphics and decorates the hallway leading to his indoor swimming pool with them, but the general population still not only shakes its head in disapproval, but takes a hostile, if not downright hate-filled view of it. Any visit to a museum will convince one of this. This is even the case with the guards there. One doesn't need to be a prophet to say that this sort of art will never become popular. In fact, it did achieve some social distinction, particularly in the Weimar Period, and it favored depictions of the simple life; but did it for this reason become popular? Hardly. The fishermen it depicts will not—unlike the industrial magnate just mentioned—hang expressionistic graphics on the walls of their houses. There is a well-known anecdote about Munch: once, when he was in financial need, he tried to pay a workman with an etching. The workman took it and wrapped something up in it.

What is the reason for this disparity? What doesn't conform, especially as it appears in the deformations which are characteristic of this art, is an annoyance to our natural way of looking at things, which expects something that conforms. This annoyance is in not in any sense something superficial but has its roots deep in the essence of the matter and points to antinomies which are not so easily resolved. Artistic seeing is not, as is often thought, merely an intensified natural seeing, any more than philosophical thinking is an intensified natural thinking or poetic language an intensified natural language. The differences here are not "gradual" but "general." The public is no less right in its judgement than the artist who inevitably finds himself in opposition to the public with his productions, if he isn't willing to compromise himself. The opposition here becomes even more widespread and sharpened in the case of the visual arts—painting and sculpture—where, unlike, for instance, with music, everybody without further ado considers himself to be responsible and believes he can and should pass judgement. For the eye is the favored sense for perceiving reality, and reality is for the public mind concreteness. The extent to which a work of art copies concreteness is therefore its unquestioned and indisputable measure. No amount of explanation, no matter how much one has tried and continues to try, will ever remove this measure.

Expressionism was, however, more than a new movement in art, just as its goals were not merely aesthetic and formal. Rather, it strove for a "complete renewal of the human condition," and, corresponding to the altered world, sought to express a new realism. "Twilight of Humanity" is the characteristic title of a representative collection of poetry (and at the same time reveals its tie to Nietzsche in its early period).

Faced with the work of one of its most eminent exponents, Max Beckmann, Kubin opined that, "sometimes the heart stands still. Nay, our time" is "forced to distill its beauty from terror."[9]

Terror—of what? Of what doesn't conform to the world, of the "unspeakable senselessness of life," as Beckmann confesses in a war letter (Sept. 24, 1914), of the "insanity of the cosmos," as the same Beckmann notes 36 years later a few months before his death in view of the Korea crisis at that time.

But not only terror of that. If Beckmann today "is considered one of the most important German artists of the 20th century, if not . . . the most important," and one asks oneself on the occasion of a Beckmann exhibition, why (*Beckmann-Ausstellung*, Kunstverin Hamburg, 1979), so I think it is that, by his own avowal, ultimately at issue in his painting is "over and over again capturing the magic of reality," which "constitutes the genuine mystery of existence," and that means, in view of the "radical dialectic" which "his work is based on," nothing other than making the nonconformity of the real visible. And it is about this—not about conformity and inconformity of things and of societal relations—that we shall be speaking here. And I must ask you to follow trains of thought which I hope will not tire you through their abstractness and which can only invoke their untimeliness as an argument for their timeliness.

While conformity designates the essence of the world generally—one of the oldest names for it is *cosmos, ordo,* order—the accent in nonconformity falls on the first part of the word, on the non, "not."

Here would be the place to deliver a eulogy on the not. On the not, not on the nothing. If we could not say not, we could not speak or think at all. The not is the most basic linguistic and logical act. One thing is contrasted with another through the not. But the not is capable of incomparably more. Through the not language voices in language what lies outside and beyond it. By virtue of the not we can raise ourselves above the finite, we can, for example, say, "It is not any of these things," and inwardly view, so far as it is possible, what defies thought: that everything is not everything and nothing is not nothing.

The first, "It is not any of these things,"[10] would once again be an example of a naïve statement; the second, everything is not everything and nothing is not nothing, would be an example of a dialectical statement, whereby characteristic for this dialectical statement is the way the nots accumulate in it and how it makes use of them.

We can distinguish worldly inconformity from the nonconformity of the real by there being in the case of the former an underlying unity, just that unity which is world, in the case of the latter none.

For: there is no opposition, as deep-going as it may be, without an underlying unity. This elemental principle of logic and ontology has unrestricted validity for the world; for the real it has no validity at all. And it is just this experience

---

[9] Quoted in *Der Zeichner und Grafiker Max Beckmann* (Kunstverein in Hamburg, 1979), p. 4.
[10] Struve discusses this thesis in *Philosophie und Transzendenz: Eine propädeutische Vorlesung* (Freiburg: Verlag Rombach, 1969), pp. 83ff., beginning in a section entitled: "The Nihilism of the General Understanding." (Tr.)

that evokes the horror and the fright we are speaking of. Fright is: to fly out of one's seat. Fright can also be joyful. No reality without taking fright. In certain extreme moments of inner clairvoyance and clarity we become aware in a lightning flash that the authentically real—reality in the ultimate sense—of which we, of which every thinking being equipped with consciousness would like to know at any price what it is, not only withdraws itself from our understanding, from our will and perception, but we have become aware that these relational concepts or any other kind of concepts cannot be applied to them, that they have so to speak nothing to say there, that thought will be of no avail with respect to reality.

The dilemma that presents itself here should in no way be removed. Once we have perceived it, we may so little disregard it as is tolerable. That seems to go against all logic and against the speculative understanding. But now we are speaking naïvely; we are not yet reflecting, but are only seeking to clarify the perception of this difference.

We do not mean by nonconformity that the real is "incomprehensible," "inexplicable," "unknown," "wholly other." When I understand and represent in this way I myself can still hole up in the ultimate and in fact do so; I can so to speak withdraw into myself as into an ultimate fortress and in this way encounter the terror of that which is unfathomable in thought. Rather, the experience of the nonconformity of the real signifies the breaking down and the coming to naught of my conceiving, and that means at the same time of my conscious I before reality as naked thereness.[11] In such a moment I perceive that it is not even indifferent to me, but has nothing to do with me. The terror of this horror characterizes all human thought and perception when it comes into its own.

Now it is our task to explicate this more closely and to document it and, so far as possible, to overcome the countless instances of inner resistance, which at the same time activate misinterpretations.

Every metaphysical experience has, as an intellectual and for this reason as a temporal and finite experience, a history. In a universal late epoch, such as is the one we live in today, we are tremendously burdened with this history, but we can in place of that survey whole other spaces than those who came before us could, and all assertions have moved into our horizon through scholarly research in connection with modern means of communication and storage in a manner and to an extent such as never before in the history of mankind.

We can today therefore no longer restrict ourselves to a Western body of thought, though it needn't for that reason come to bad exports and imports. As far as thought itself goes, we can also learn many things from the East without having or being obliged to give up our own essential character, as, for instance, through persistent practice, spanning centuries in uninterrupted continuity, spiritual and inner energies can be released and enhanced in a measure which is for

---

[11] See *Spuren und Stürze*, #141: "That which shows itself when you cancel yourself—the not of yourself—und when you immerse yourself in nature—the not of the world—: the there of reality." See also #217: "The there—What is of me is not there, but in me." (Tr.)

us unimaginable.

Thus, I would like to cite a series of historical testimonials to the experience in question first of all from Eastern, then from Western cultural spheres. In no respect can I in so doing achieve completeness; I pick out only a few examples, among them examples not usually picked, but which perhaps precisely for that reason speak to us more than the others.

The first testimonial that I'd like to adduce is admittedly just as meaningful as it is famous. It originates from ancient Indian thought: it is a poem on the origin of the world and belongs to the later hymns of the *Rigveda* (X 129). The *Vedas* themselves are considered the oldest linguistic monuments in India. I give the text in the verse translation by Paul Deussen, which still has not been surpassed by any of the later translations, aside from the fact that most of them seem to be dependent on his. We also have Deussen, the important indologist and classmate of Nietzsche's from *Schulpforta*,[12] to thank for a detailed interpretation.[13] Deussen thinks this hymn is "perhaps the most admirable piece of philosophy to come down to us from ancient times."

It begins with a narrative so to speak of the primal cosmic condition as follows:

> At that time not-being was not, nor being,
> There was no realm of air, no sky beyond. —
> What covered in? And what gave shelter?
> Where was the deep abyss? Where the sea?
>
> Death was not then, nor was there immortality,
> Night was not then, day was not apparent. —
> That alone breathed windless in freshness of its origin:
> Apart from it was nothing else.

One senses, if one finds the quiet to let verses like these sink in, an inner proximity to the sensual reality of the cosmos, which we of today no longer have nor could have, bare nature long since having become distant to us.[14] Call to

---

[12] We read in *Wikipedia*: "Pforta, or Schulpforta, is a former Cistercian monastery, Pforta Abbey (1137-1540), near Naumburg on the Saale River in the German state of Saxony-Anhalt. It is now a celebrated German public boarding school, called Landesschule Pforta. It is coeducational and teaches around 300 high school students." (Tr.)

[13] *Allgemeine Geschichte der Philosophie mit besonderer Berücksichtigung der Religionen*. Von Dr. Paul Deussen. 1. Band, erste Abteilung: *Allgemeine Einleitung und Philosophie des Veda bis auf die Upanishad's*. 4. Aufl. Leipzig: F. A. Brockhaus. 1920 (Vorrede zur 1. Aufl. 1894; 2. Aufl. 1906), pp. 126-127. See pp. 119-127. [My translation of Paul Deussen's translation, freely using Ralph T.H. Griffith's 1896 translation, at sacred-texts.com, and the unnamed translator's translation at http://www.wsu.edu/~wldciv/world_civ_reader/world_civ_reader_1/rig_veda.hhtm. (Tr.)]

[14] One is reminded of D. H. Lawrence when he said that the ancients were living "breast to breast, as it were, with the cosmos, in naked contact with the cosmos . . ." and: "We

mind that at that time no electric light burned, not to mention neon lights. Neither did the houses have oil heaters, nor did one watch television in the evening. There were neither cars, which disturb the silence of the night, nor tourists, who today penetrate into the most remote regions and damage their integrity. When one thinks that everything has really always been the way it is now, it can hardly be believed.

At the same time the stanzas of this hymn are extremely artistically fashioned: in each stanza "the first and second half face one another like chorus and rival chorus" (Deussen) and the progression of the whole seems like a "drama," which culminates in the fourth stanza and then once again in the singular closing.

In the first two lines of the fourth stanza the philosophical primal seed and germ of knowledge that being arises from utter not-being through longing *(kama, eros, love)* is given voice, as the preceding stanzas narrate. And how do we know that? The next two lines of the stanza give the answer:

> Sages searched in the heart's appetites
> And found existence rooted in not-being.

"Heart"—one could also say in German "*Gemüt*."[15] The epistemological foundation of this decisive knowledge thus lies in our inmost core's being one with the inmost core of reality, and therefore our being able to find the origin of being by going deep into ourselves.

But now comes something extraordinary, the dramatic course of the hymn. Its last two stanzas increasingly put the knowledge gained in question, ending finally in total *aporia*:

> Yet who has succeeded in perceiving
> Whence comes this creation?
> The gods arose after this creation!
> Who knows then whence it first came into being? —
>
> He, the first origin of this creation,
> Whose eye surveys this world in highest heaven,
> Whether he formed it all or did not form it,
> Surely he knows it! — or does not even he know it?

This hymn was written down more than two and a half millennia ago. I

---

have lost the cosmos, by coming out of responsive connection with it, and this is our chief tragedy." *Apocalypse* (written 1929-30, publ. posth. 1931—New York: The Viking Press, 1966), p. 159f. and p. 42. (Tr.)

[15] The German word *Gemüt* in Kant's day could be used to mean "mind" and is usually so translated. Today the affective elements have come to the fore, as in *gemütlich*, "cosy," "comfy," "jovial." The word is formed with the collective prefix *ge-*, which intensifies the word, and *Mut*, "courage," "valor," "mettle," as the word *Gebirge*, "mountain range," "mountains," is formed from *Berg*, "mountain." (Tr.)

don't believe we have become any wiser in the matters it speaks of or have anything essential to add to what it says. One can place the accents differently in interpreting it. A recent anthology, *Aus Religion und Literatur* (Insel Verlag, 1983) offers, along with a confusing misprint, only the first two stanzas and leaves out the remaining five. Deussen sees the culmination in the fourth stanza, where the knowledge of love (*kama*), as the deepest nature of things, is gained. Certainly not unjustifiably. But the message, unmatched in its penetration and denseness, lies in the last line of verse, which the hymn closes with:

> Surely he knows it! — or does not even he know it?

That is to say: The gods don't enter into consideration for the question concerning the origin of the world. They arose "after the creation" and can know nothing about this. Only the creator and sustainer, whose eye, as it says, "surveys this world in highest heaven." He knows it. And then the tremendous question, with which the whole thing ends: "Or does not even he know it?"

The questioning retraction of the ultimate knowledge gained is not some agnosticism, as one often reads. "Thus the poet begins as a theist and ends almost as an agnostic."[16] To make this clear is of great importance. One understands under agnosticism according to the relevant formulations "the doctrine that true being cannot be known." A classic formulation of an agnostic position would be, for instance, Protagoras's well-known utterance:

> About the gods I admittedly have no possibility of knowing either that they are or that they are not or what sort of form they have; for there is much that hinders knowledge: that they cannot be perceived and that the life of men is short.

It would be agnosticism if our hymn had said: he, who made the world or didn't make the world, in any case covers it in or holds it in his care—he knows it. We, on the other hand, don't know it. But that possibility is excluded because our "heart" is one with the innermost core of things. What comes into view here is something far worse and deeper, namely that the real, reality in the ultimate sense, isn't merely inaccessible to knowledge and the understanding or that it transcends them, but that it is so to speak oppositional in form to them, and the nameless horror, which is inseparable from the recognition of this fact, becomes perceptible in the last question. This horror und this terror further are marks of that Indian religious and philosophical thought, which in terms of expanse and intensity has exercised an unrivaled effect on the consciousness of mankind, namely Buddhism so-called. More important than its doctrinal contents may well be the stance of consciousness it generally takes up, and which distinguishes it entirely, at least in its early form, from the modern and from the Western outlook on things.

---

[16] *Epics, Myth and Legends of India: A Comprehensive Survey of the Sacred Lore of the Hindus, Buddhists and Jains.* By P. Thomas (Bombay o. J.), p. 12.

The originator of this thought received the title "the Buddha," in loose translation "the Enlightened One" or "the Awakened One." As few historically verified facts about his life as have been passed on by tradition, and as much as transfiguring legend knows to report, everywhere in the texts of the later canon an unmistakable, unique personality, just as forceful as it is likeable, comes to the fore, and the characteristic quality of the Buddha's personality is how he experienced that terror and, without lessening or softening it, endured it and came to terms with it.

After his enlightenment at the age of 35, this "Awakened One," accompanied by *bhikkus*, "beggers," that is, monks, wandered about northeast India proclaiming his insights, though he remained in a fixed location during the rainy season. It seems important for right understanding not to get any wrong ideas about the Buddha's "teaching activity." Just two passages from the canon, whose genuine historical core no one would doubt, will suffice to cast a bright light on the matter, more than long dissertations could:

Concerning the wandering, a talk on the "Happiness of Disentanglement" closes as follows:

> What time, Nāgita, I reach the high road and see no one either in front of me or behind me, I have leisure even to urinate and to defecate.[17]

And as for the question about what he does during the rainy season, the Buddha lets it be known, not, as one might think, that he instructs the monks or something like that, but:

> Sunk in mindfulness of inhaling and exhaling, friends, was the Sublime One wont to tarry during the rainy season.

For by no means did the originator of this thought, after having won the decisive knowledge, feel compelled immediately to teach others. Rather, he only did this after overcoming considerable inner resistance and always with a great deal of reserve. Was it not the case in accord with his intention that each seek for himself to attain enlightenment? And he was innately not a "founder of a religion," even if he was an excellent teacher.

Characteristic of early Buddhist teaching are generally three factors:
- The point of the teaching is that everyone must know and realize himself by himself. No one else, not even the Buddha, can do it for him.
- This point is nothing more than the wholesome.
- The differentiation and tolerance of the teaching, that it, as it says, "is with difference and not one sided."

---

[17] Translated from the German translation in *Die Lehrreden des Buddha aus der angereihten Sammlung . . .*' Band IV, page 181 (*Anguttara Nikāya* VIII, IX, 86), and blending it with the English translation in *The Book of Gradual Sayings* IV, page 227. (Tr.)

No command is absolute, not even that of chastity, though breaking that rule would result in the monk's being thrown out of the order.[18] As far as the single-minded interest in wholesomeness is concerned, one could think, looking at it from a Western perspective, that Buddhism is pragmatic. But that would be too simple because wholeness or salvation is not only meant in a worldly sense but is related to the terror we spoke of before.

Having made these preliminary remarks, I shall now discuss, with the brevity offered us within the limits of this lecture, a fundamental distinction in Buddhist meditation, which is of great importance for our topic.

Meditation is a foreign word, which indeed today has largely been emptied, just as ambitious as it is worn out, and can include everything possible and impossible. Yet perhaps in its widest sense it will be able to lead us to what is intended here.—That meditation—spiritual exercise and immersion which goes beyond natural objective reflection—is the basis of older Buddhism, in fact of Indian thought generally, doesn't need to be elaborated further. Accordingly, this is also where it is most difficult for Western man to penetrate. Prerequisite for all meditation is exercise in higher morals. This too cannot be elaborated further here.

Buddhist meditation unfolds now into two great branches or areas. The one—the Pali and Sanskit term for it is *samadhi*—is inner collectedness, absorption, immersion. It takes place in four levels, as they are over and over again presented in the canon without alteration, and lead finally to a state of total inward inner peace and equanimity (*samatha*). It is important to notice that this state, a temporary liberation from the world and its distractions, by the nature of things can only be a temporary one. As a liberation from the world it is related to the world, is "mundane," not "transcendental," and can be reached by anyone willing to make a commensurate effort.

Things are different with insight, clear-seeing[19] (*vipassanā*), by which the other great branch of meditation is known and which is the prerequisite for entry into nirvana and is thus transcendental in kind. It means, as presented by the Buddhists, the intuitive, immediate insight, like a flash of lightening, into the misery, transitoriness, I-lessness and substancelessness of all formations of existence, into the fact that these are "processes which in their essence are foreign" to me and to which applies: "That does not belong to me, I am not that, that is not my I."[20]

Vipassanā—insight, clear-seeing—means nothing other than the intuitive comprehending of what we have here been calling the nonconformity of the real. There is nothing "that is," including myself, that would conform to the real. This clear-seeing is like a flash of lightning, is not temporary, and means an alteration

---

[18] See on this the instructional talk in *The Book of Gradual Sayings* X 75.
[19] According to http://www.experiencefestival.com/a/Vipassana_-_Etymology/id/1869130, *vipassanā* means "see apart or discern; deep seeing." (Tr.)
[20] *Pali-Buddhismus in Übersetzungen*. By Karl Seidentücker. Zweite vermehrte und verbesserte Auflage. (Oskar Schloss: München-Neubiber 1923), p. 276.

of life forever. That there are such transformational insights is borne witness to, in the Western sphere for instance, by Nietzsche's flash of insight into the eternal return, and much light can be shed on this thought from here.

If one ponders this distinction, which is fundamental to Buddhist thought, and examines its discussion in modern Buddhist literature, one will also see what the difficulty with it is, and with that we have come to the narrower topic of our lecture.

"Insight," "clear-seeing," "intuitive flashes" and whatever the numerous designations may be—what is meant by them?

In any case, not an "objective," object-laden knowledge of any kind. For no object without a subject. The subject in the sense of I-think has been left behind. This is already the case with *samatha*-meditation. It's not a question of a representation of a thinking I, but rather of direct insight into the nonconformity of all representations generally with the real in the absolute sense.

Buddhist teaching makes an important distinction, to wit, between "truth, manner of expression, explanation valid in the highest sense" (*paramattha-sacca*) and "conventional truth" (*vohara-sacca*).[21] This distinction isn't about a "double truth" in our sense, but about the one truth's being expressed differently depending on the ability of the listener to comprehend what is being said.

When we speak of insight, clear-seeing, here this is completely a "conventional" mode of expression, already recognizable in our being able, even if with some difficulty, to place what we have been explaining into a framework of ideas and concepts familiar to us. In the strict and highest sense we cannot speak of this, but just the same we cannot pass over it in silence.

The famous concluding sentence of Wittgenstein's *Tractatus Logico-Philosophicus*, "What we cannot speak about we must pass over in silence,"[22] is not applicable to the *aporia* which the nonconformity of the real places us in.— One runs across this concluding sentence of Wittgenstein's first work often. It gets its meaning only from the differentiated investigations that precede it. By itself, isolated, it is on the one hand something commonplace and on the other hand a silence like this is a literary one. For I cannot also say that I must totally pass over in silence what I am passing over in silence.[23]

Before we go further into the difficulties which present themselves here and which obviously are bound up with the subjectivity of thought—every thinking requires a thinker—let us first cite a few testimonials from the Western sphere.

How does it stand with Plato, the father of philosophy when we take that

---

[21] *Buddhistisches Wörterbuch von Nyanatiloka*. Zweite, revidierte Auflage. Herausgegeben von Nyanaponika, (Konstanz 1976).

[22] Translated by David F. Pears and Brian F. McGuinness (Oxford: Routledge, 1961). (Tr.)

[23] Struve has reflected on this statement a number of times. The last time he does, it is with an intensification: "When we cannot speak, we cannot also say that we cannot say it, but we are struck dumb. Not: are silent. For silence is still a speaking, indeed, often a more powerful speaking than with words." *Spuren und Stürze: Aufzeichnungen aus Skizzenbüchern 1984-1987*, #260. (Tr.)

word in the singular Greek sense which it received from him, placing his stamp on all subsequent philosophy? The nonconformity of the ultimately real was by all means experienced by Plato—how could it be otherwise?—and found expression in language. Indeed, always only very succinctly and briefly and in such a way that he turns away from it—similar to Parmenides of Elea before him—but for just that reason all the more forcefully. He especially does this when he critically reflects anew on the foundations of his philosophy of ideas at the beginning of the second phase of his thinking. I'm thinking particularly of the first position of the dialectical part of his *Parmenides* dialogue, where in a grandiosely planned exhibition, which to this day has never been surpassed, the thought of the absolute in the strict sense is developed, and the investigation concludes: "Consequently, it can neither have a name nor be spoken of, nor can there be any knowledge or perception or opinion of it.—Apparently not.—Neither can it be named nor spoken of, nor be an object of opinion or of knowledge, nor perceived by any creature.—It seems not.—Now can this possibly be the case with the (absolute) One?—I, at least, do not think so."[24]

Some think this shocking conclusion is to be taken in the sense of a "negative theology," because it comes out that nothing at all can be known or asserted about the absolute; others take it to mean that this thought should be carried *ad absurdum* because the whole thing seems to end up in meaningless contradictions.—In my view neither the one nor the other is the case, but rather we are dealing with nothing less than a demonstration of the nonconformity of thought with reality in the absolute sense. Plato turns away from that in the following second position and turns towards the world.

I would like to cite Meister Eckhart as another witness from the Western world. It is a great advantage to have someone who speaks our (German) language, and that in a stage when it was still fresh and unmutilated. His German sermons bear witness in certain extreme passages to uttermost and ultimate inner experiences with a power of language and penetration that haven't seen their like. Or where else has one said and dared to say, "For that God is God—he has that from his immoveable detachment, and from his detachment he has his purity und his simplicity and changelessness."[25] And in the same place, "Bear in mind . . . that God's creation of the heavens and the earth affected his detachment as little as if he had not made a single creature."[26]

In the German word *Abgeschiedenheit* [detachment, disinterest, seclusion]

---

[24] *Parmenides* 142 a. Here I translate Struve's translation with an eye on Francis M. Cornford's in *Plato and Parmenides* (London: Routledge & Kegan Paul, 1939), p. 129, and the Greek. In Zürich, Struve studied mathematics with Andreas Speiser, whose commentary, *Ein Parmenideskommentar*. (Leipzig, 1937), both Struve and Cornford used. (Tr.)

[25] Meister Eckhart. *Die deutschen Werke*. Herausgegeben und übersetzt von Josef Quint, Band V (Stuttgart, 1963), p. 412.

[26] Blakney, p. 85. I base my translations of Eckhart starting with this one on those by Blakney, *Meister Eckhart: A Modern Translation* (New York: Harper and Row, 1941), changing them to match Struve's translations. (Tr.)

is *Abschied*, "farewell, parting." Parting [*scheiden*] is going away. "*Homo Mysticus*" is one who goes away. Away—not towards and beyond—is the essence and mystery of meditation, as is Buddhist nirvana. (The prefix "nir" in nirvana means "out, forth.")[27] Parting means leave, abandon, to give up the relation to what one leaves. Total lack of relation cannot be grasped conceptually. Departure is a mystery just like reality; detachment is its site.

Eckhart was also a great eulogist of the not, after him again Suso and later Angelus Silesius. At the end of his sermon *Renovamini spiritu mentis vestrae* we read, "For if you love God as a god, a spirit, a person, or as if he were something with a form—you must get rid of all that. 'How, then, shall I love him?' Love him as he is, a not-god, a not-spirit, apersonal, formless."[28] And in the sermon *Ego elegi vos* (and similarly in several other sermons), we read, "It is a species of the divine order, it is in itself one and has nothing in common with anything else. Many great priests fumble it."[29] The inconformity of certain passages of his sermons with Church doctrine led, as is well known, to a deadly conflict.

In the sermon *Convescens praecepit* Eckhart says, "Wan daz ist gotes eigenschaft und sin nature, daz er unglich si und niemanne glich si."[30] One can translate passages like these into Modern High German in various ways. The question is how one places the accents, and minimal divergences in translation can mean a world of difference in understanding. Quint translates the decisive word, *unglich*, with "*ohnegleichen*" ["without comparison," "unique," "without his like"], as did Büttner before him, "Das ist Gottes Eigenheit und Natur, daß er ohnegleichen ist . . ." That is uplifting and edifying, even full of wit, but also nothing more. Schulze-Maizier translates: *unvergleichlich* ["beyond comparison," "without comparison"].—But to our ear Eckhart's assertion is harsher and absolutely offensive; it doesn't say that God is beyond comparison or without his like, which would ultimately be banal, but gives expression to a difference whose horror is felt everywhere in those passages from the sermons where he presses forward to the ultimate. And that this occurs is what makes these sermons unique. To this end I would like to close this discussion with another passage, "But I shall go further and say what must sound strange: I am speaking in good truth and in the eternal truth and in the everlasting truth that this light ("the little spark in the soul," the "*seelenfünklin*") is not satisfied by the simple, still, motionless essence of the divine being . . . it wants to penetrate the simple core, the still desert, into which no distinction ever crept—neither Father, nor Son, nor Holy Ghost; in the innermost part, where no man is native, where it is satisfied by that light, there it is more inward than it is in itself."[31]

---

[27] *See* Helmuth von Glasenapp, *Die Weisheit des Buddha* (Baden-Baden, 1946), p. 126.
[28] *Meister Eckhart*, ed. by Franz Pfeifer (Leipzig, 1857), p. 320. [Blakney, fragment 42, p. 248.]
[29] Meister Eckhart. *Die deutschen Werke*. Herausgegeben und übersetzt von Josef Quint, Band II (Stuttgart, 1971), p. 66.
[30] Ibid., p. 89. [Blakney translates, ". . . for it is God's property and nature to be incomparable and like no one." p. 196 (Tr.)]
[31] Ibid., p. 420. [Blakney, fragment 39, p. 247 (Tr.)].

"Da nieman heime enist." One senses in passages like these that Eckhart is who he is. Quint translates, "*wo niemand daheim ist*" ["where no one is at home"]. The older folk will remember the rallying cry, "Home into the *Reich*." "The German *Wehrmacht* brings the German lands home into Adolf Hitler's *Reich*," was the headline over a series of pictures in the *Illustrierter Beobachter* of October 6, 1938, which by chance recently came into my hands. One would have expected that the light of the soul, when it so to speak pushes forward and into ultimate reality, comes home, but it comes rather to where "no one is native."

Native, at home—one could in turn also say, at one's house [*zu Hause* = "at home"]. There, where no one is at his house. Reality—unlike the world and being— is not a house.

Let us finally cast a glance at the one in whose thought the entire Western intellectuality is one more time reflected and recapitulated and even takes account of Eastern thought, at Friedrich Nietzsche, and we will see, as could not otherwise be expected, that the horror of facing the nonconformity of the real to everything we think and believe pervades the gamut of his notes and writings, from early essays like "On the Pathos of the Truth" on to late and very late pieces such as "How the 'True World' Finally Became a Fable"[32] and finds expression in an unheard of ways in these writings, now loudly screaming, now softly whispering, now pathetic, now coldly sober, calling into service all the means of language with a virtuosity and reflexivity which probably hasn't seen its like in this way in the literature of the world.

Rather than providing several quotations by Nietzsche, one famous posthumously published note from his later period on his first book, *The Birth of Tragedy*, will suffice: "Very early in life I took the question of the relation of *art* to *truth* seriously, and even now I stand in holy terror in the face of this discord."[33]

It is true that this note has been quoted so often that it has virtually become a commonplace in the literature on Nietzsche, and it has been interpreted and thought through so often as apparently to render it empty. Yet the immensity that is Nietzsche radiates from it without any diminution.

Discord, conflict [*Zwiespalt*], "splitting in two" [*Zweispaltung*]—we associate dispute [*Zwist*], dissention [*Zwietracht*], between [*Zwischen*]—is used preeminently in the sense that one is in conflict with oneself. The conflict between art and truth—in our terminology: between world and reality—is no external or outward conflict, but one which runs through Nietzsche, one which is most inwardly torturous.

Entsetzen [horror, terror] means literally "to remove one from one's peaceful domicile and possessions." The sensuous meaning is still there when we say, *eine Festung wird entsetzt* [a fort is relieved from enemy forces]. *Entsetzen* is

---

[32] Translated by Walter Kaufmann in *The Portable Nietzsche* (New York: The Viking Press, 1954), p. 485f. (Tr.)

[33] Friedrich Nietzsche. *Nachgelassene Fragmente 1887-1889*. 16[40] paperback ed. p. 500 (translated looking at Krell's and Magrini's translations). (Tr.)

the antonym of *besetzen* [occupy].

Nietzsche characterizes this horror as holy. Like all such words he uses, this too scintillates with the most diverse contrasts. In Part Three of the first volume of *Human, All Too Human*, titled "The Religious Life," Nietzsche says of the holy man that "he *signified* something that exceeded all human measure."[34] "Holy horror" apparently means something twofold: the horror goes beyond all human measure, but is for that reason also salutary.[35] And in the end no word of Nietzsche's is spoken that doesn't spring from this intention.

We read in *Ecce Homo* at the beginning of the section "Why I Am a Destiny": "I have a terrible fear that one day I will be pronounced *holy*: . . . I do not want to be a holy man; sooner even a buffoon. . . . Yet in spite of that . . . the truth speaks out of me.—But my truth is *terrible* . . ."[36] With passages in Nietzsche like these it all depends on *how* what is said is said. "My truth is terrible"—anybody can say that. As an objective thesis it seems over the top, sentimental, ridiculous, a harbinger of insanity. But in the way it is said, the terrible announces and bears witness to itself in unprecedented fashion in its push towards expression.

Finally, here would be the place to draw attention to the significance the concept of the absurd gains in Kierkegaard and later in French existentialism, particularly in Sartre and Camus. However, while in Kierkegaard everything he utters and thinks is explicitly referred to transcendence, this has fallen by the wayside with the latter and gives the feeling of the absurd its own peculiar atmosphere of inescapable dullness such as no earlier yet so radical skepticism knows.

As far as Kierkegaard is concerned, modern religious philosophy, following him, especially in the chapter "The Absolute Paradox" in *Philosophical Tidbits*,[37] developed the concept of the "wholly other." It was Rudolf Otto who in epoch-making manner developed this concept in his book *The Holy: On the Irrational in the Idea of the Divine and its Relation to the Rational*. (This book appeared in 1917(!) and in 1936 saw its 25th edition.)

In the transition to the last part of my lecture I would like to make a few comments on this book. Rudolf Otto coined and developed there the concept of the numinous. Romano Guardini argues against Rudolf Otto in his important lecture "*Die religiöse Sprache*" and says in regard to the concept of the wholly other, "Otto has not thought purely from the phenomenon here but from certain previously made decisions. Were the numinous really wholly other than the worldly, it couldn't attain givenness at all. Already the judgment, 'it is other

---

[34] Translated by Walter Kaufmann and R. J. Hollingdale in: *On the Genealogy of Morals and Ecce Homo*, edited by Walter Kaufmann (New York: Vintage Books, 1967), p. 173. (Tr.)

[35] *Heilbringend*, the word used here, contains *heil*, "sound," and *Heil*, "salvation," the same root as in heilig, "holy," and Heiliger, "saint" or "holy man." (Tr.)

[36] Translated by Walter Kaufmann in: *On the Genealogy of Morals and Ecce Homo*, edited by Walter Kaufmann (New York: Vintage Books, 1967), p. 326. (Tr.)

[37] On the translation of the title, see above p. ixf., note 8. (Tr.)

than everything worldly,' presupposes that there is a receptivity for its experience and a comparable level for judgement on this."[38]

Is Guardini right? Yes and no.—Certainly the concept of the "wholly other," when I understand it in ultimate precision, so to speak cuts itself off. As soon as I try to think and to speak about the wholly other, I have already deprived it of its otherness in the ultimate sense. But, thought strictly, I cannot even say this. And Guardini's objection annuls itself logically just as much as Otto's concept.

One will hardly do justice to Rudolf Otto with formal logical objections. That is also not Guardini's concern, but what he's really charging Otto with is that he emphasizes the "gulf" between the "numinous" and the "worldly" too strongly, that rather a "double relationship" exists: "the numinous can express itself in every element of the world, but it is also hidden by the world."[39]

We think rather, just the opposite, that Rudolf Otto does not sufficiently express the difference of the "Wholly Other" from the worldly, and herein lies the unsatisfactoriness and dated quality of the book. It is not that we now simply need to radicalize the otherness of the numinous. Nothing would be gained by this, and logic would rightly oppose it. What is unsatisfactory lies rather in that Otto—unlike Kierkegaard in *Philosophical Tidbits*—objectifies the "wholly other" to the "numinous"[40] at the outset and makes it an object of a scholarly treatise. No matter how much verve he may write this with, and no matter how much he may be on guard against "both trivializing and finally extirpating the fundamental religious process" through systematization, this is just what he does.

Nonconformity of the Real means that the real is not only wholly other than the usual worldly, but that the reflexive experience of the I and everything that proceeds out of it into thought and action breaks down before reality in the sense of naked thereness and comes to nothing. This is what the terror and the horror that is more or less expressed in the historical testimonials cited earlier is about and can always be sensed with tremendous urgency. It goes to the ultimate root of the natural feeling of the I and concerns the apparent inseparability of I-hood and the understanding.

This should, time allowing, be discussed in more detail. The problems surrounding the intimate connection between the understanding that thinks and the reflexive experience of the I, as is well known, has intensely occupied Western philosophy from Descartes, Spinoza, Leibniz on through Kant, German idealism: Fichte, Hegel, Schelling, and on through to Kierkegaard and Nietzsche, and has been thought through in an increasingly radical manner in the phases indicated by the this enumeration of names.—It has also intensely occupied Eastern

---

[38] *Die Sprache. Fünfte Folge des Jahrbuchs Gestalt und Gedanke.* Herausgegeben von der Bayerischen Akademie der schönen Künste (München 1959), p. 19.
[39] Ibid., p. 20.
[40] See Rudolf Otto, *The Idea of the Holy: An Inquiry into the Non-Rational Factor in the Idea of the Divine and Its Relation to the Rational,* translated by John W. Harvey (London: Oxford University Press, 1923, 2nd ed. 1950), p. 29.

thought, though in a different manner and form. The Vedantic creation hymn discussed earlier ends with the unthinkable alternative that how the world came into being is not knowable at all, not even by a being equipped with a supreme intellect. The central thought of older Buddhism is that the natural I-consciousness is illusory.

First we need to see the indissoluble connection between I-hood and the understanding as it is set forth by Kant in a manner just as thorough-going as it is valid. Already Descartes showed that all thinking is an I think, that there is no thinking without a subject that thinks. (And the computer? It doesn't think. It stores data and calculates.) Descartes showed further that the I that thinks can at any time come back upon itself. All thought is not only an I think, but at the same time an I think that I think, and this indissoluble connection is for Descartes the fundament of all certititude and with that, of philosophy. Kant formulated this with unsurpassable precision in the famous sentence of his *Critique of Pure Reason*: "It must *be possible* for the 'I think' to accompany all my representations . . ."[41] The representation of the I think is, as Kant says in the same passage, an "act of spontaneity," and what accomplishes this act is combination. That means: the I in the I think is the source point of the understanding, and its essence is combination. But combining presupposes not only something to combine, but also a unity which precedes it, or, as we've been putting it, a primordial conformity of the things to be combined.

One could say in general that intellectuality is that which conforms. Where there is no conformity, there can be no intellect, and with that also no I in the sense of the I think. When the real as that which does not conform announces itself, it so to speak takes the breath away from the one thinking in me: it becomes torpid and dies away.

The real experienced in that way is not "beyond all reason." "Beyond all reason" is itself a construction and invention of reason. That the real does not conform to it doesn't also, for example, mean that it is without reason. With such statements I am acting on the assumption that there is some ultimate conformity of myself as a thinking being with reality, just as the natural and accustomed feeling of the I draws on what is intellectual to a much greater extent and depth than one usually—once again, intellectually—means.

Let us try from another angle to make what we mean clearer: what I apprehend intellectually I objectify. Without that the intellect can comprehend nothing. There are as many and as diversely-natured types of I as there are types of objects; the intellect objectifies each and every thing on its own and, when it extends this activity to ultimate realities, it falls into the contradictions, to have shown and solved which Kant justifiably viewed as the greatest achievement of his philosophy.

But not only do I objectify what I comprehend intellectually, but at the same time I posit it and myself in relation to it as real in such a way that my re-

---

[41] *Cr. of P. R.* B 131. [*Critique of Pure Reason*, translated by Norman Kemp Smith (New York: St Martin's Press, 1929). (Tr.)]

ality depends on its reality, not the other way around, so that what has been posited as real can threaten or also support me. Something relatively analogous occurs in nightmares and wish-fulfillment dreams. If I wake up, I annul the positing of reality which has been accomplished there with relief or disappointment, but in any case with a sense of liberation.

What I have once posited in a wakeful state as real remains so for me, even if I refrain from it or forget it. Just as this positing was carried out by me, so also it can be annulled, canceled[42] only by me. No one else can do it for me.

"Positing" and "cancelling" show themselves thus to be ultimate intellectual and inner enactments. How things stand with one generally depends on how things stand with these enactments.

To posit something as real is an act of spontaneity, not mere arbitrariness. Otherwise what has been posited wouldn't have the binding character that it has for me. If positing were mere force, it wouldn't have that binding character. Rather, in positing, freedom and necessity constitute a unity. For just this reason, one can only cancel what one has posited oneself. And, on the other hand, there is no cancelling without previously having posited.

Positing reality in this sense pertains to belief, not knowledge and judgement, indeed, occurs ultimately against my better judgement. For when I am fully mindful, there is nothing that I can posit as real. Mindfulness thereby proves itself to be the "transcendental," the highest virtue. This is already the case in older Buddhism.[43]—Belief admits of no doubt. I do not doubt what I believe. As soon as I doubt, belief has been annulled.

Let us approach this from yet another angle. For the intellect, only that is believable and possible which it itself participates in, which it can in some way enact and create. It is only such things that it can posit as real. Since the real itself is uncreated and cannot be created, it is necessarily the unbelievable and the impossible for the intellect. Since we cannot be indifferent to the real, the intellect must deny it. The intellect is therefore in relation to the real always a "nihilist." *The wonder of the real*—the unbelievable and the impossible—doesn't exist for it.

The creation of objects, the transcendental activity of the intellect, is necessary. Only by this activity can I assert myself as an intellectual being over against the sensuous impressions that impinge upon me and master my natural life. This activity does indeed mean a separation of subject and object, but this separation is not a "split," the way it is commonly conceived. It is then also not experienced as something negative or of lesser importance. To be sure, I do ex-

---

[42] *tilgen—The New Cassell's German Dictionary* gives: extinguish, blot out, abolish, eradicate, obliterate, efface, erase, extirpate, destroy, exterminate; cancel, annul; amortize, pay off, redeem (New York: Funk & Wagnalls, 1958). This is an important word for Struve: he came up with this word, as the context indicates, as the opposite of *setzen*, "posit." (Tr.)

[43] *See* on this: *Der einzige Weg: Buddhistische Texte zur Geistesschulung in rechter Achtsamkeit.* Aus dem Pali und Sanskrit übersetzt und erläutert von Nyanaponika (Konstanz 1956).

perience it as negative that I accept and posit the objects created in this way as real. This, in fact, I do naturally—that is, as soon as I'm not completely mindful—but it is not necessary like the creating of objects.

Rather, everything truly intellectual, everything "spiritual," begins with my no longer enacting such positings of reality, and, since as I begin to be aware of myself I find myself confronted by a whole world posited by me as real, everything truly intellectual only begins when I begin to cancel these positings.

And the first positing to cancel is the one by which I posit myself as real.

Canceling oneself seems difficult, impossible, absurd, and the understanding, when this cancelling is expected of it, rebels against it in every way, becomes offended.—Cancelling oneself is the great mystery because one annuls oneself without annihilating oneself. Annihilating oneself is utter nonsense. In the absolute sense, one can so little do this as one can hoist oneself into the air by one's own hair.

Instead of cancelling oneself, one seeks naturally—that is, as soon as one is not mindful, is not perceiving oneself—to enhance and to perfect oneself. In general, we prefer to attain perfection in order to support ourselves on the idea that we are its perpetrator and proprietor and thereby so to speak absolute. But the real is not the perfect. How could it be that, if it is that which does not conform?

Yet, why such assertions, and why such knowledge? So that we grow smarter and more clever? But there are so many who are more clever than we. That's not it.—So that we can gain a final answer? But that there is no such thing, neither within everything, unless for use in the world, nor outside everything, is just what follows from the insight into the nonconformity of the real with respect to us and our representations.—But it does not follow in the way that I can once again gain a final answer in the recognition that every final answer and the I that gains it is imaginary. With that recognition one hasn't yet freed oneself from the spell of the imaginary. Rather, one must endure the horrible which is inseparable from this insight, without lessening or mitigating it, until it unfolds its wholesomeness in such a way that it compels one to leave the domain of such assertions altogether. For one cannot pit truths against illusions. Illusion is so powerful and sweet that nothing temporal can oppose it; on the contrary, ultimately everything just reinforces it. But one can cancel the impulse to form illusions. That occurs in an entirely different sphere from the one where illusions have an impact on things. That horror [*Ensetzen*] displaces [*versetzt*] one into this sphere.

What is the inner constitution of a person displaced and horrified in such a way? That is what I would like to adumbrate briefly in conclusion. There are two things which chiefly characterize it: mindfulness and trust, both not in a general and vague sense, but in a very particular and specific sense, taken in the sense required by the previous discussions. As such they are the highest virtues: mindfulness allows us to become aware of the real: trust establishes the relation to it.

Mindfulness is generally, as was set forth earlier, the virtue of virtues. For only through it can the impulse to illusory formation of the I along with everything that follows from that be cancelled and annulled. But where this occurs, there is no longer anything that one could find in one's inmost self that one could support oneself on or benefit oneself by.

How is this to be endured? It can only be endured when something else is added: trust. It is no less significant than mindfulness. For if the real cannot be measured by any measure, as is the case if it is that which does not conform, then my relation to it can only be that of naked trust. This trust is not for that reason blind, but follows from my experiencing the real directly in its nonconformity with everything that I think and am as that which belongs to me intrinsically, and that means infinitely.

Without mindfulness and trust there can be no awareness of the real and no passage to it. Without passage to the real there can be no affirmation and sufficiency: the goal of every inner enactment.

Select Bibliography of Publications by Wolfgang Struve

Book Publications

Die neuzeitliche Philosophie als Metaphysik der Subjektivität: Interpretationen zu Kierkegaard und Nietzsche. Symposion, Band 1, 1948, 207-335

Wir und Es: Gedankengruppen. Zürich: Max Niehans, 1957.

Der andere Zug. Salzburg-München: Stifterbibliothek, 1967/69.

Philosophie und Transzendenz: Eine propädeutische Vorlesung. Freiburg i. Br.: Rombach Hochschul Paperback, Band 7, 1969.

Übergehn zur Wirklichkeit: Philosophische und andere Reisenotizen. Salzburg: Stifterbibliothek/Bad Goisern: Neugebauer Press, 1970.

Unglaubliche Wirklichkeit: Philosophische und andere Reisenotizen. Salzburg: Stifterbibliothek, 1972.

Homo Mysticus: Zwei Vorträge. Wies/Südschwarzwald: Anders Leben, 1983. (Includes "Welt und Wirklichkeit. Überlegungen zu einer elementaren Unterscheidung im philosophischen Denken" and "West-östliche Mystik und das Problem absoluter Transzendenz.")

Über die Nichtkonformität des Wirklichen. Wies/Südschwarzwald: Anders Leben, 1986.

Spuren und Stürze: Aufzeichnungen aus Skizzenbüchern 1984-1987. With 4 watercolor paintings by the author and an afterword by Ursula Schneider. Vienna: Passagen, 1999.

Publications in Journals and Books

Review of Johs. Jensen, *Plotin. Gnomon.* 22, (1950): 181-182.

"Über das 'Ergo' in Descartes' 'Ego cogito, ergo sum' und 'Sum, ergo Deus est.'" *LEXIS: Studien zur Sprachphilosophie und Begriffsforschung,* Vol. II, no. 2 (1950-51): 239-262, 'Nachtrag' on p. 238.

"Das deutsche Kierkegaard-Studium." *Meddeleser fra Søren Kierkegaard Selskabet,* Copenhagen 3, no. 1 (1951): 79-84.

"Eine geschichtliche Erinnerung zum Thema: 'Erfahrung und Metaphysik'" (on Plato, *Phaedo* 79a). *Proceedings of the XIth International Congress of Philosophy,* Vol. IV, *Experience and Metaphysics* (1953): 128-133.

"Kierkegaard und Schelling." *Orbis litterarum,* Tome X, Copenhagen (1955): 252-258.

"Sigbjörn Obstfelder." *Neue Zürcher Zeitung.* 188, no. 18. (Juni 1967).

"Japanische Reisenotizen." *Handschreiben der Stifterbibliothek.* No. 47. Salzburg 1967.

"Frühjahrslapplandreise 1967." *Handschreiben der Stifterbibliothek.* No. 48. Salzburg 1967.

"Gedankensplitter." *Handschreiben der Stifterbibliothek.* Nr. 71. Salzburg 1972.

"Magie der Stille." In *Alles Lebendige meinet den Menschen: Gedenkbuch für Max Niehans,* 41-47. Bern, 1972.

"Welt und Wirklichkeit: Philosophische Reflexionen." *Scheidewege: Vierteljahresschrift für skeptisches Denken,* 2 no. ½ (1973): 162-183.

"Kierkegaard und das existenzielle Denken." *Scheidewege: Vierteljahresschrift für skeptisches Denken,* 3 (1973): 162-183.

"Die Engadiner Pastelle von Stockhausen." Vorwort zum Katalog der Ausstellung: *Hans Gottfried von Stockhausen: Eine Werkübersicht.* Galerie der Stadt Esslingen am Neckar. Villa Merkel. 7. Juni bis 3 Juli 1983.

Translations

Blaise Pascal. *Vom Geist der Geometrie*. With Introduction. German translation with French text *en regard*. Darmstadt: Claasen & Würth, January 1948.

Sören Kierkegaard. *Johannes Climacus oder de omnibus dubitandum est*. With Introduction. Darmstadt: Claasen & Würth, December 1948.

Works of Struve translated into other languages

Philosophie und Transzendenz: Eine propädeutische Vorlesung. Translated into Arabic by Abdel-Ghaffar Mikkawy with a foreword by Wolfgang Struve. Cairo 1975. A second edition appeared in 2012.

"Kierkegaard und Schelling." Translated into Japanese by Eiko Kawamura. *Kierkegaard-Studiet*. No. 13 (1983): 57-63.

On Wolfgang Struve

Rudolf Brandner. "Die Rehabilitation philosophischer Mystik. Zum Gedankenwerk des Philosophen und Mystikers Wolfgang Struve." *Mesotes*, 3 ,no. 2 (1993): 249-262.

Markus Enders. *Transzendenz und Welt: das daseinshermeneutische Transzendenz- und Welt-Verständnis Martin Heideggers auf dem Hintergrund der neuzeitlichen Geschichte des Transzendenz-Begriffs*. Frankfurt am Main: Peter Lang, 1999.

References

World and Reality

Lecture, held in the Philosophische Geschellschaften of Zürich and Berne in May 1974 and in the Studium Generale of the University of Freiburg in June 1977. Unpublished.[1] In part summarized in: Till Beckmann, *Studien zur Bestimmung des Lebens in Meister Eckharts deutschen Predigten* (Frankfurt am Main – Bern: Peter Lang, 1982), pp. 101ff.

Mysticism East and West and the Problem of Absolute Transcendence

Lecture, held in the Studium Generale of the University of Freiburg in June 1980 and at a conference of the Marie Gretler-Stiftung at the University of Zürich in November 1980. Printed in the *Herderbücherei Intiative* 42, ed. by Gerd-Klaus Kaltenbrunner, 1981. The editor cut out the last part and provided titles and headings. The lecture appears here in unaltered form.

On the Nonconformity of the Real

Lecture, held in the Studium Generale of the University of Freiburg i. Br. on June 18, 1984.—I would especially like to thank Mr. Peter Giovanazzi for bringing this to the press.

---

[1] That is, prior to its German publication in *Homo Mysticus*. (Tr.)

www.ingramcontent.com/pod-product-compliance
Lightning Source LLC
Chambersburg PA
CBHW052135300426
44116CB00010B/1910